PROPERTY OF:
NEWPORT BEACH PUBLIC LIBRARY
NEWPORT CENTER LIBRARY
856 SAN CLEMENTE DRIVE
NEWPORT BEACH, CA 92660
(714) 644-3191

In the Driver's Seat

MW00355667

PUBLIC LIBRARY

IN THE DRIVER'S SEAT

THE NEW CAR BUYER'S NEGOTIATING BIBLE

W. JAMES BRAGG

RANDOM HOUSE
NEW YORK

Property of:
NEWPORT BEACH PUBLIC LIBRARY
Newport Center Library
856 San Clemente Drive
Newport Beach, Cal. 92660

Copyright © 1993 by Fighting Chance®

All rights reserved under International and Pan-American Copyright Conventions. Published in the United States by Random House, Inc., New York, and simultaneously in Canada by Random House of Canada Limited, Toronto.

Library of Congress Cataloging-in-Publication Data

Bragg, W. James
    In the driver's seat : the new car buyer's negotiating bible / W. James Bragg. — 1st ed.
      p.   cm.
    Includes index.
    ISBN 0-679-74633-1 (pbk.)
    1. Automobiles—Purchasing.   2. Negotiation.   I. Title.
TL162.B73   1993
629.222'029'7—dc20   93-992

Manufactured in the United States of America

First Edition

New York   Toronto   London   Sydney   Auckland

Neither the author nor the publisher warrants that purchasers or readers of this publication will be able to buy any specific vehicle for any specific price. We provide information that we believe will be helpful in the negotiation process, but the result will be determined by the actions of individual shoppers and the supply and demand conditions in the market.

This publication is designed to provide accurate and authoritative information, as of press time, in regard to the subject matter covered. It is sold with the understanding that the publisher is not engaged in rendering legal, accounting or other professional service. If legal advice or other expert assistance is required, the services of a competent professional should be sought.

DEDICATION

- To every man who's ever bought a new car or truck and wondered whether the next guy got the same vehicle for a lot less.

- To every woman who's suffered through the purchase process and wondered whether she was a victim of gender-based price discrimination.

- To every member of a minority group who's wondered whether he or she has encountered race-based price discrimination when buying a new car or truck.

- To everyone who's about to buy that first new vehicle and wonders whether he or she will end up asking the same questions.

This book is for all of you. After reading it, you'll wonder why no one ever told you this before.

Contents

If a little knowledge is dangerous, where are those who have so much as to be out of danger?
        —Thomas Huxley

Among new car buyers, it's those who've read this book.

Introduction

I f another book covered the subject well, we wouldn't have written this one. These are the '90s, and the automobile business has changed dramatically in the last few years. As the cover promises, *In the Driver's Seat: The New Car Buyer's Negotiating Bible* is loaded with inside information that will empower you in today's automotive market—much of it information you won't find in any other book.

OUR SUBJECT IS MONEY, NOT CARS

There's an old maxim that applies here. We call it Life's 80/20 Rule. Simply stated, it says that 20 percent of the people account for 80 percent of the activity, no matter what the subject. (For example, 20 percent of movie-goers buy 80 percent of the tickets; 20 percent of readers buy 80 percent of the books.)

When the subject is the money dealers make from selling new cars, the rule says that 20 percent of the customers account for 80 percent of the profits. And when we walk into that showroom, every car salesman views every one of us as a prime candidate to join that unfortunate group. This book's reason-for-being is to keep you out of that group.

The one sure way for anyone to avoid getting taken is to become an informed and disciplined shopper, period. This book can help you become that shopper. We will not be steering you to any specific car or truck. You are the best judge of which vehicles fit your requirements.

And we are not experts on fuel economy, or safety, or reliability, or maintenance and repair costs, or insurance ratings. These important issues are well covered in lots of all-purpose books and magazines.

Our focus here is primarily on the elements impacting the *financial* outcome of the purchase process—elements those all-purpose books and magazines cover only superficially. Our job is to provide you with the knowledge that will give you real negotiating leverage in a transaction that traditionally has been stacked against the buyer.

We'll do that by bringing together all the relevant information, distilling and synthesizing it into one coherent presentation. We'll demystify the automotive purchase process thoroughly (in English, not AutoSpeak) and teach you how to use that information to negotiate from a position of strength, in the driver's seat.

EIGHT SUBJECTS YOU'LL BE GLAD WE STUDIED

To illustrate, here are eight important aspects of today's market reality—things you must know about to deal from strength, but areas no other book covers adequately.

1. Today the average vehicle has over $1,000 built into its price for incentives—customer rebates, reduced-rate financing offers and secret factory-to-dealer incentives. Since you'll pay for them, you ought to be informed so that you can benefit from them. This book not only teaches you how to bargain for that incentive money, it even provides a mechanism (via an 800 number) for you to get a current listing of manufacturer offers when you're ready to start serious shopping.

2. Four import manufacturers—Peugeot, Sterling, Daihatsu and Yugo—left the U.S. market in 1991 and 1992. We believe others will join this exodus before the decade ends. And some makes that remain here will lose dealers as their sales continue to decline. These issues have potential financial and convenience implications that everyone should consider before buying a new vehicle. Yet you'll never see them covered by the media, which can't risk alienating dealers and manufacturers and losing those advertising dollars. Chapter 12 places them front-and-center.

3. Recent research shows that, compared to Caucasian males, women and minorities, who buy more than half of all new cars, face significant price discrimination in the purchase process—discrimination that may cost them over a billion dollars a year. This book presents these research results in Chapter 2 and proceeds to teach its readers how to turn the tables. (No other book we've seen even mentions this landmark study.)

4. The fortunes of auto companies and their dealers ebb and flow from month to month, impacting each make's flexibility on price. Disappointing sales typically lead to excess inventories and a greater willingness to deal. Chapter 3 explains this in detail, and Chapter 25 provides a mechanism for you to get a current sales and inventory picture to help you identify the more vulnerable makes.

5. Leasing now accounts for about 20 percent of passenger car purchases. Other books dismiss leasing as a bad idea unless you qualify for tax write-offs or have more money than time. *That's dated advice.* With manufacturer-subsidized offers, leasing can be a very attractive alternative for almost any creditworthy buyer. Chapter 22 is, hands down, today's bible on leasing.

6. GM's Saturn subcompact has become a roaring success, and several hundred other dealerships have adopted Saturn's one-price, "no-dicker" sales policy. But these Saturn wannabes don't have Saturn's crucial pricing umbrella working for them, and they don't offer the consumer the same pricing reassurance. Chapters 13 and 14 take you behind the curtain for a revealing look at how "no-dicker" pricing really works.

7. Ford and Chrysler improved their basic warranties dramatically

with the 1992 models, from 12 months/12,000 miles to 36 months/36,000 miles. More than one third of new-vehicle purchasers buy a Ford or Chrysler product, and this change should influence their decision to purchase an extended warranty contract. Chapter 19 covers the subject completely.

8. The Customer Satisfaction Index (CSI), a relatively new advertising staple for makes that score well in national surveys, also has implications for your shopping behavior. Manufacturers now conduct surveys to rate each of their dealers on customer satisfaction, and you should want to buy from a dealer with an above-average CSI score. Chapter 19 teaches you how to identify those dealers.

Our objective is to make this the most comprehensive, interesting and useful information package available for helping new-car and -truck shoppers save money. We won't talk down to you or tell you things you already know (such as, Dress comfortably but conservatively when visiting showrooms). We'll just explain, as simply as we can, how the process works, and how you can take advantage of it, instead of letting it take advantage of you.

COMPLETING THE LOOP: FIGHTING CHANCE®, A UNIQUE INFORMATION SERVICE

To negotiate successfully, you'll need the most current vehicle-specific information for the cars or trucks on your short list. When you're ready, our company, Fighting Chance, offers you an easy way to get that data by calling an 800 number or writing to us, if you wish. The Fighting Chance information package includes the factory invoice pricing for the vehicle or vehicles you're shopping, a current report on manufacturers' incentive programs (including factory-to-dealer cash offers) and an updated sales and inventory picture for each make. See Chapter 25 for ordering details.

After you've purchased your vehicle, we'd like to know if you think this book has helped. Like the auto manufacturers, we're always working to improve our product, and we'd welcome your comments and suggestions. Send them to Fighting Chance, 5318 East 2nd Street, No. 242, Long Beach, CA 90803.

In a time of turbulence and change, it is more true than ever that knowledge is power.
—John F. Kennedy

Everybody's Problem: An Uneven Playing Field

Quick! Can you name three things that are more fun than driving home in a brand-new car or truck? For most people, that's a tough call.

Now, can you name three things that are less fun than shopping for and negotiating the price of that new car or truck? For most people, that's even tougher.

We all suffer world-class anxiety in this process, with good reason. For years, car prices have been going up much faster than take-home pay. In

1992, the average new car's actual transaction price was over $17,600. That's more than six months' wages for a typical household, enough to make anyone anxious. And there's no relief in sight.

Despite a sluggish economy, fragile consumer confidence and projections that new-vehicle sales will remain well below their mid-1980s levels well into the 1990s, you can expect the automakers to continue hiking prices. The increases for General Motors, Ford and Chrysler may average only a "modest" 3 percent, but that's more than $500 a year.

The Japanese Big Three—Toyota/Lexus, Honda/Acura and Nissan/Infiniti—can no longer count on strong yearly sales increases in Japan. Economic weakness at home, combined with political pressure to avoid escalating U.S. trade tension further, has forced them to shift their focus from increasing market share to increasing profits. Which means increasing prices, probably in the range of 4 to 6 percent per year.

The domestic makes should see this as an opportunity to gain a pricing advantage and recapture some market share from the Japanese. But they lost so much money in the early 1990s that they may react by simply cutting their incentive offers somewhat, effectively raising prices again.

What's the prognosis for the consumer? *The average new car will sell for over $20,000 by the middle of the decade.* Is it any wonder that many of us would rather visit a dentist for root canal work than visit a showroom to shop for a new car or truck?

THE REAL PROBLEM: AN UNEVEN PLAYING FIELD

The gut-level issue, of course, is that the price of that expensive machine is *negotiable,* and therefore different for each buyer. By contrast, the price of just about everything else we buy is firmly established, and therefore the same for each buyer. That puts the pressure on us. We've got to do something we're not used to doing: negotiate the price of the second most expensive purchase most of us will ever make. And we're operating on unfamiliar turf, in a position of weakness, because we do it only once every few years.

But those salesmen we have to negotiate with are on very familiar turf, the car store, and in a position of strength, because they do it every day. (Yes, they call the dealership "the store." There are more than 22,000 of them nationally, and the average store for a Top Six automotive brand moves 500 to 900 new cars and trucks each year. Many sell thousands!)

Those salesmen are trained to do one thing really well: maximize the car store's profit on each sale by separating us from as much money as possible. Their job is to determine how much is "as much as possible" for each prospect and, if the number is high enough, to close the sale at that price before the prospect gets away.

We make that job easier than it should be by giving them lots of important information they can use. We tell them exactly which car we want, and how much we can pay per month, and which vehicle we're trading in. In return, they give us no information we can use, such as how much that car really cost them, how low they'll really go to sell it, and what our trade-in is really worth. As a result, a playing field that was uneven from the start tips even further toward them. And when the transaction is over, most of us don't know whether we got a good deal or got taken.

EVERYONE DESERVES A FIGHTING CHANCE

As a *Motor Trend* writer said in a recent annual auto review issue, "Negotiating with terrorists is easier than bargaining with car dealers." That's why we wrote this book. We wanted to give the average new-vehicle shopper a fighting chance by making the playing field a little more level.

Our goal is to make the purchase process less painful and costly for you. To do that, we must change something important in that process. Since we can't change those salesmen and what they do, we've got to help change you and what you do.

THE OBJECTIVE: TO MAKE YOU MORE
KNOWLEDGEABLE THAN THE CAR SALESMAN

That's not Mission Impossible. The average car salesman isn't that knowledgeable. He's trained to qualify, control and close most of the people who walk in, prospects who just don't know much. But he's not well prepared to control and close people with solid knowledge of his business, a well-planned, disciplined approach and insights that even he may not understand. Those shoppers can have real negotiating leverage.

(Incidentally, when we say salesmen, assume we mean both sexes. There are successful auto saleswomen, but the male stereotype is still the dominant factor. Also, when we say cars, assume we're referring to both cars and trucks.)

How can we make you more knowledgeable than the car salesman? By giving you the attitude, facts, up-to-date insights and advice you need to negotiate from a position of greater strength.

We can't guarantee, of course, that you'll save hundreds or thousands more with this information than without it. That's up to you and what you do with it. The supply and demand conditions in your market for the vehicles you're interested in will also influence the outcome.

But remember, knowledge is power. The main advantage the salesman has over most buyers is that he thinks he's got all the knowledge. If you absorb the information we give you, you'll know more than most car salesmen. If you act on this information, you'll go into the process with real confidence in your ability to negotiate effectively. And if you believe you can, you will.

NO PAIN, NO GAIN

Most people work harder planning a $2,000 vacation than planning the purchase of the $20,000 car they'll be vacationing in for years. Why? For two reasons: (1) Planning a vacation is more fun; and (2) they know how to plan a vacation, but they don't know how to shop for a car. If smart shopping were easy, everyone would do it.

The facts say everyone doesn't. Incredible as it seems, in the J.D. Power and Associates 1989 Early Buyer Study[sm], *about 40 percent of new-car buyers nationwide actually admitted to paying list price or higher!** And we'd bet many of the other 60 percent paid more than they realized, simply because they weren't focused on all the ways a car store can make money on a deal. (More on this in Chapter 5.)

Smart shopping requires homework. Studying this book and acting on it intelligently will require more of your time than simply going out and buying a car next Saturday. The trade-off is between time and money, perhaps as much as several thousand dollars.

We'll assume that you wouldn't have bought this book if you weren't willing to trade time for money. Let's get on with your education.

---

*J.D. Power and Associates, *The California Report*, April 1990.

*Everything is funny as long
as it is happening to
someone else.*
　　　　—Will Rogers

2

The Other Problem: Price Discrimination

Our civil rights laws focus on the areas of employment, education, housing and public accommodations. When it comes to the prices we pay for the things we buy, there's a comfortable assumption that good old American competition at the retail level tends to eliminate price discrimination.

Try telling that to women, who know they pay more for shoes than men do for theirs, even when the materials and workmanship are the same. Or to inner-city residents, who know that stores in their neighborhoods often charge higher prices for lower-quality goods than similar stores else-where.

Women and minorities will not be surprised to learn that they also face significant price discrimination in the automotive marketplace. *We believe a conservative estimate of the cost of this discrimination is over a billion dollars a year, compared to the prices paid for the same vehicles by white males.*

WOMEN MAKE THE WHEELS GO ROUND

The female working population has grown dramatically over the last two decades, sparking a revolution in auto design and marketing strategies. With three out of four women between twenty and fifty-four years old in the labor force, women have become a key target for automakers.

Manufacturers now spend as much money researching women's auto-motive needs as men's, with good reason. Women purchase half of the new passenger cars sold and about one quarter of the light trucks, which include some very profitable segments (such as minivans like the Dodge Caravan and sport-utility vehicles like the Jeep Grand Cherokee).

Many vehicles are designed to appeal primarily to women. The all-new 1993 Ford Probe is a perfect example; its design team was supervised by Ford's first female designer. This sporty coupe segment, which is aimed directly at women, also includes the Honda Prelude, Mitsubishi Eclipse, Geo Storm, Nissan NX, Eagle Talon, Mazda MX-3, Toyota Paseo, Hyundai Scoupe, Plymouth Laser, Nissan 240SX and the convertible Volkswagen Cabriolet.

The auto manufacturers have changed their ways to satisfy the needs of this powerful new economic force; they treat women differently from men. As a result, both win. Women get the products they want, and manufacturers sell more new cars and trucks.

The automakers' franchised *dealers*, however, are another story. Most women have always suspected that new-car salesmen treat them differently than men and that, as a result, they end up paying a different price from men—a higher price. That's why many of them drag along their husbands, boyfriends or fathers when they shop.

Many members of minority groups have suspected they face similar price discrimination.

Now there's irrefutable evidence that substantiates these suspicions.

THE SEARCH FOR THE SMOKING GUN

Ian Ayres, a professor at Stanford Law School and a research fellow of the American Bar Foundation, was interested in testing the ability of competitive market forces to eliminate gender- and race-based price discrimination in markets not covered by civil rights laws. Since a new-car purchase represents a large investment for most consumers, he saw the retail automobile market as "particularly ripe for scrutiny."

Between the summers of 1988 and 1990, when he was an associate professor at the Northwestern University School of Law, he conducted research to examine whether women and minorities were at a disadvantage in the process of negotiating the price of a new car.

He trained several college-educated testers of different genders and races to negotiate in the same way for specific models. They conducted 180 independent negotiations at 90 dealerships in the Chicago area, bargaining to each dealer's "final cash offer." To eliminate other financial considerations, no trade-in vehicles were involved.

THE FACTS OF PRICE DISCRIMINATION

The smoking gun wasn't hard to find. The results were published as the *Harvard Law Review*'s lead article in February 1991. They demonstrated that retail car dealerships systematically offered substantially better prices on identical cars to white men than they did to white women and African-Americans.

Specifically, final offers to white women contained about 40 percent more dealer profit than final offers to white men. Offers to African-American men contained more than twice the profit, and African-American women had to pay more than three times the markup of white male testers.

The tendency to charge African-Americans higher prices was echoed in this comment one dealer made to Professor Ayres: "My cousin owns a dealership in a black neighborhood. He doesn't sell nearly as many [cars], but he hits an awful lot of home runs. You know, sometimes it seems like the people that can least afford it have to pay the most."

The study also revealed that testers were systematically steered to salespeople of their own race and gender, who then gave them *worse* deals than others received from salespeople of a different race and gender. (Consumers tend to feel more comfortable with someone of their own race and gender; salespeople take advantage of that implied trust and sell them higher-profit deals.)

The major conclusions of this initial study were confirmed by a subsequent larger-scale test involving four hundred additional negotiations in the Chicago area.

THE IMPLICIT ASSUMPTIONS BEHIND THE FACTS

Professor Ayres hypothesizes an explanation for this price discrimination. While there's no way to prove it, we think he's right on the money. Here's the essence of his reasoning:

• The dealer's objective is to maximize profits on each sale. (That's the American way, right?)

• The natural outcome of the bargaining process is that identical vehicles are sold to different buyers at different prices. Dealers make little or no profit on some sales, but a great deal of profit on others.

• The less the competition with other dealers for a given sale, the more profit the dealer is likely to make on the transaction.

• If a dealership can infer that some prospects are less likely to shop at other dealerships—because they aren't well informed about the dynamics of the retail automotive marketplace, or because they can't spend the time required, or because they simply hate the entire bargaining process and just want to get it behind them—that dealership is more likely to view these prospects as potential patsies for high-margin transactions. And that dealership is more likely to conclude that it can safely charge these prospects higher prices.

• Like it or not, our society is still rife with stereotypes about women and minority groups that provide at least a subconscious rationale for salespeople to view them as more likely candidates for high-margin, slam-dunk, sucker deals. Here are the most obvious:

> *Women and minorities have less time to shop around for competitive bids.* Compared to white men, they are less likely to be able to take time off from work to shop without losing wages. And women are more likely to have family responsibilities that further restrict their shopping time.

> *Women and minorities are less sophisticated about the auto shopping process.* They are less likely to seek out informa-

tion about the realities of the retail market and to understand that the sticker price is negotiable. They will be more passive in the sales situation, less likely to negotiate aggressively. That will make it easier for the salesperson to control the outcome.

Women, in general, are more averse to the entire bargaining process. Haggling over the price of a new vehicle is a competitive ordeal. Some men relish the battle; for them it's one of the last macho things they can do without a gun. Most women simply hate it. They'll pay a higher cost just to get it behind them.

THE LIGHT IN THE TUNNEL

Women and minority readers shouldn't be discouraged by these revelations. The purpose of this exercise is to get into the opponent's brain, to understand what's in there. The good news is, that's just about all that's in there.

And is the salesman going to be surprised when he meets you! Because you're going to shake his faith in those implicit assumptions, confusing him and neutralizing his offense. He'll try all his tricks, but you'll be that knowledgeable, disciplined shopper we promised you'd become, and they won't work.

The road from here to there begins on the next page. It's straight and clearly marked.

3

The

Big

Picture

In early 1992, an IBM sales representative in Milwaukee contracted with a dealer to buy a new Dodge Viper, Chrysler's limited-production sports car, for $2,500 over the suggested retail price. When the vehicle arrived, the dealer sued the customer to get out of the contract. According to The Wall Street Journal, *he thought he could sell it for as much as $20,000 over the sticker price! On learning of this embarrassing incident, Chrysler's executive vice president for sales and marketing lamented, "We have to change the entire culture of our franchise."*

Any deal you make will be influenced by two things that have nothing to do with you: the overall state of the automobile market, and the specific supply and demand conditions for the vehicle you want.

Since the auto sales climate is one of the most overreported subjects in journalism, getting up to speed starts with simply keeping your eyes and ears open. As you think about new cars or trucks, pay attention to those monthly sales reports on the TV news, in your local paper, or in national media like *The Wall Street Journal* or *USA Today*. They'll give you a general feel for how eager dealers are to sell new vehicles.

What you really want to know, however, is how eager some specific manufacturers and dealers might be to sell the vehicles you're interested in buying.

THEIR WEAKNESS IS YOUR OPPORTUNITY

The retail automobile business is driven by momentum, both the overall market and the fortunes of each specific make. After a precipitous three-year decline, total new-car and new-truck sales improved modestly in 1992. But they were still well below the weak level of 1990, and no one is predicting a smooth return to the glory days of the mid-1980s. In this difficult environment, many makes have watched their sales and market shares wither, while others have developed the tough competitor's ability to weather any storm.

The smart shopper understands that these differences create buying opportunities, and that you should be able to negotiate a better deal with those who are most eager to sell.

CHECK THE CHART

Turn to the Appendix and the Big Picture chart on page 169. This kind of information can make you a smarter shopper by giving you a feel for the relative performance of the different auto makes. Assume that the chart shows the current status of sales and inventories for each make. (It doesn't, since we created this hypothetical information just for this exercise, but it serves a purpose. Later, we'll tell you how to get a similar chart showing actual current information when you're ready to start shopping.)

As you'll see on the top line, through the first five months of the model year, new-car sales are down 6 percent from the previous year. But truck sales are up 6 percent, leaving total new-vehicle sales down about 2 percent. With numbers like these, it's safe to assume that dealers are really scrambling to move metal. It's a buyer's market . . . for the smart buyer.

The two columns on the left side of the chart show each brand's sales performance compared to that of the total market, using a range of five general classifications. If an individual make's sales are up or down about as much as the overall market, we rate its performance as "average."

Relatively stronger performance is rated as either "above average" or "excellent"; weaker results are either "below average" or "poor."

The two columns on the right show relative inventory levels by make, using five general classifications that range from "low" to "very high." For perspective, industrywide levels tend to fluctuate throughout the year in a range from roughly a 55-day supply to about a 75-day supply. For most manufacturers a two-month supply is an ideal target, providing the vast majority of buyers with sufficient color and equipment choices. Inventories higher than that usually increase costs much more than they do sales. Whenever they approach the three-month level, you can bet that the costs of financing that supply are hurting both the manufacturers and their dealers. Those makes should be more vulnerable to smart, informed shoppers.

As the chart illustrates, the overall market inventory is average for cars and high for trucks. (Note that the truck category includes minivans, sport-utility vehicles and full-size vans, as well as pickup trucks.)

Check the makes you are interested in. Is their sales performance better or worse than their key competitors' and the total market? Are their inventory levels relatively higher? As a general rule, dealers selling makes that are doing less well, with higher inventories, will be more willing to deal aggressively on price than those selling makes with relatively better sales and lower inventories.

To be more specific, let's assume that you're in the market for a passenger car and you're considering comparable models from Subaru, Nissan and Toyota. Here's what the chart shows about each:

	Sales Performance Compared to Total Market	Inventory Levels
Total Car Market	–6%	Average
Subaru	Poor	Very high
Nissan	Above average	High
Toyota	Excellent	Low

Considering their relative sales and inventory positions, which of these makes do you think is likely to be most flexible on price? Subaru, naturally. Which is likely to be least flexible? Toyota.

Given their relatively high inventory levels, it is also likely that both Subaru and Nissan are offering customer and/or dealer incentives. (We'll discuss incentives in a later chapter.) Even without extra incentives, however, the Big Picture suggests that the average shopper is likely to strike a better bargain with either of them than with Toyota.

There's another important side to the Big Picture. When demand is down for new cars, it's usually up for used cars. And with fewer new-car buyers to provide late-model trade-ins, the supply of good used cars is down. That suggests it should be a seller's market for a nice, clean trade-in . . . for a smart seller. We'll cover the implications of this later, in Chapters 7 through 9.

When you're ready for serious negotiating, you'll want a current version of the Big Picture chart, along with the data on the current dealer invoice price of the vehicle or vehicles you're considering, and an up-to-date listing of manufacturers' incentives for both the customer and the dealer. All three elements are included in a package that you may order directly from us. Ordering details are in Chapter 25.

4 Attitude

Adjustment

Necessity never made a good bargain.
—Benjamin Franklin

ere are three basic principles of automotive negotiating that you must burn into your brain. Think of them as three legs of the stool that will transform you attitudinally from a potential pushover into a tower of strength.

PSYCHOLOGY 101

This is a serious competition. It may seem relatively civilized, but it's definitely you against them.

One of the primary rules of this competition is, Don't give your opponent a psychological advantage. Which is exactly what you'll do as soon as you show him that you're emotionally attached to any specific vehicle. As soon as he knows that, he's dealing from a position of greater strength. And you'll end up paying more for the car simply because he knows you have to have it.

Car salesmen are trained to make the purchase process as emotional as possible. Decades of experience have confirmed that they get more money from emotional people than from cool, rational shoppers.

How do you avoid this trap? *By projecting total emotional detachment.*

In the showroom, on the lot and during the test drive your behavior should say, A car is a car, something that gets me from Point A to Point B. Lots of cars will do that, including many that this store doesn't even sell. I'm going to check them all out and buy the best deal.

(Ask your friends who shop for antiques about the "Don't-let-'em-know-what-you-really-want-as-soon-as-you-walk-in" rule. They'll tell you it also works well at estate sales, swap meets and garage sales.)

That doesn't mean you can't fall in love. Just don't let the salesman know until you've completed the transaction. At your price, not his.

> HEAVY BREATHING SHOULD BE RESERVED FOR MORE APPROPRIATE OCCASIONS. IN CAR STORES IT LEADS ONLY TO HEAVY PAYMENTS.

ANATOMY 101

Look down at the floor right now. That's where you'll find the most powerful negotiating tools you'll ever own: your feet.

The only thing a car salesman dreads more than selling you a car too cheaply is watching you walk out of his store, into the arms of another salesman at another store. He's got bags of tricks to keep you there for hours. (Dealers sometimes *require* that their salesmen *not let you leave* without seeing a sales manager!)

If you think you're being pressured, or he's not listening to you and moving in the direction you want, tell him politely that he's wasting your time . . . and leave. (A funny thing happens if you walk; it actually *improves* your leverage when you return later, because he'll know you're someone who'll walk again if things aren't going your way.)

> ONE REASON GOD GAVE YOU FEET WAS TO WALK AWAY FROM CAR SALESMEN.

REALITY 101

A study by a respected British consulting firm concluded that 1.3 billion cars would be built in this decade. For perspective, that would equal the total number of cars built in the history of motor vehicles. As every manufacturer has learned painfully in the last few years, building them is easy; it's selling them that's hard.

Reality is that there will be more car production capacity than car buying capacity for as long as anyone can see into the future. We'd have to take the minimum driving age down to three-year-olds for all the manufacturers to realize their sales projections for the 1990s.

Reality is that it will always be much easier for you to find someone who wants to sell a new car than for a car salesman to find someone who wants to buy one.

Trust this reality.

> **REALITY IS THAT YOU CAN WALK AWAY FROM *ANY* DEAL, OR *ANY* CAR, AND BE ABSOLUTELY CERTAIN THERE IS ONE JUST LIKE IT, AND PROBABLY BETTER, AROUND THE CORNER.**

The time is long overdue for this industry—the largest and most important industry in the world—to erase the popular idea that its No. 1 priority is to pull the wool over everyone's eyes.

—From a May 6, 1991, editorial by the publisher of *Automotive News,* the industry's weekly trade journal

The Juggler 5

When you're buying a new car, the salesman has three balls in the air, three important areas of opportunity to make money on the transaction.

• First, he can make money on the front end, on the difference between your purchase price and the dealer's cost on that new vehicle.

• Second, he can make money on the back end, selling you things like financing (with related life and disability insurance), extended warranty coverage, and dealer add-on options like rustproofing and fabric protection.

• Third, if the deal includes your trade-in vehicle, he can make money on the difference between what the car store really pays for your car and what they get for it, either by retailing it through their own used-car department or by wholesaling it to a used-car dealer.

(If it surprises you to learn that there's more profit potential in the second and third areas than in the first, you are in the group that needs this book the most.)

Think of the salesman as a juggler, trained to keep all these balls moving so fast that you can't tell which is which.

He wants to make a good profit on all three if he can. But the total gross is what counts, and there isn't a dealer alive who wouldn't give up profit on one of these balls to swing a deal if he knew he could make a killing on the other two.

The world is full of naive-but-happy car buyers who think they got a great deal because they bought "below dealer invoice." Or because they got a "fabulous trade-in allowance." Or a "big discount" on an extended warranty policy.

They watched only the ball that they were interested in. But the salesman watched them all.

We'll cover how to watch . . . and even control . . . what happens with each of these balls. But first you need an overall shopping plan.

Ninety-nine percent of the people in the world are fools, and the rest of us are in great danger of contagion.
—Thornton Wilder

6

If You Haven't Got a Plan, You Haven't Got a Prayer

The subject here isn't cars, it's your money, and how a big chunk of it will be divided between you and a car store and a bank or financing company (unless you're among the roughly one in five buyers who pays cash).

THE 80/20 RULE OF LIFE

Life's 80/20 Rule is one of those maxims that applies to just about any subject you can name. It says that whatever the activity, 80 percent of it is accounted for by 20 percent of the people. Here are some examples:

- 80 percent of the beer is drunk by 20 percent of the drinkers.
- 80 percent of the auto accidents are caused by 20 percent of the drivers.
- 80 percent of the wealth is owned by 20 percent of the people.
- *And 80 percent of a dealer's profits on new-car sales comes from 20 percent of his customers.*

Remember, the salesman's goal is to maximize profit on every deal. He gets paid to determine the highest amount a prospect might be willing to pay and to get that customer's commitment to pay it *before he or she leaves the car store.*

To that salesman, every prospect—including you—who walks into the showroom represents a potential high-margin sucker deal. (They call them slam dunks.)

To avoid waking up on the wrong side of Life's 80/20 Rule in this competition, you need a plan. Most people don't have one.

Here's the way most people approach the purchase process:

- They start by visiting car stores and getting excited about specific cars in the presence of car salesmen. (*Which is a really bad idea.*)

- Then, still in "new-car heat," they wonder out loud how they'll pay for that pretty thing, and (you guessed it) the salesman tells them how easy it'll be. (*Another bad idea.*)

- Finally, too confused to turn suddenly rational, they wonder out loud what their current car is worth in trade, and they accept the number the salesman gives them without checking it out themselves. (*More bad ideas.*)

They'll repeat this behavior at several car stores and think they're out there dealing. The lucky salesman who gets them at 3 p.m. on Sunday will make his weekend quota, and the happy buyers will drive their new car into the sunset without a clue that they are exactly the kind of prospects that every salesman dreams about.

YES, VIRGINIA, THERE IS A BETTER WAY

Smart buyers don't rely on car salesmen for any important information. They don't give them any, either. Smart buyers have a shopping plan that reverses the sequence that most people follow:

- They start by focusing on the car they've got. They know they're either going to sell it themselves or trade it in, and that the proceeds will represent an important part of the new car's down payment. So they begin by finding out how much their vehicle is really worth in their market today, both at retail and at wholesale.

- Then they decide whether they'll sell it themselves at retail or trade it in at wholesale. (They know the difference will affect the money available for their down payment.)

- Then they turn to the essential financial questions. They decide on the monthly payment they can handle comfortably, including auto insurance, which costs a lot more for new cars than for old ones. They also determine the down payment they can afford. They know that bigger is better, so they find some loose cash to add to what they'll get for their current car.

- They take all this information and shop for money before they shop seriously for a car or truck. This gives them a good fix on the maximum amount they can pay for a new vehicle, including all the miscellaneous sales taxes and license fees that many salesmen don't mention until you're committed to a price for the car. It also provides a basis for measuring the attractiveness of the financing offered by the dealer or manufacturer.

- Concurrently, they're reading articles on the vehicles they're interested in for information to help narrow their choices, and they're visiting car stores to obtain brochures and take test drives. But they make it clear from the start that they are not going to buy on those visits, and they avoid getting into any salesman's "closing room" because they know they're not ready.

- They decide on at least two or three finalists, including the trim levels and optional equipment they'd like on each. They pick their first choice vehicle and at least one attractive fallback alternative, based on both emotional appeal and rational analysis.

- Next, they gather all the information they can about what those vehicles actually cost the dealer, including the impact of any current factory-to-dealer incentives, as a basis from which to negotiate a purchase price confidently and aggressively. They also bone up on any direct consumer incentives being offered by the manufacturers.

- They do a little additional homework to determine which dealer finalists they want to approach in the negotiation stage. They recognize that some car stores can be much better places to buy than others, for reasons that have little to do with price.

• With solid knowledge of the real wholesale and retail values of their current cars, the best financing they can arrange independently and the actual dealer costs of the vehicles they want most, they plan the best way to approach several car stores with an aggressive offer.

• They understand the potential value of proper timing, especially in relation to incentive programs, and they plan their approach accordingly.

• They review the basic tricks salesmen are likely to use to boost their store's profits, including all the high-cost/low-value add-on options they'll try to sell, and they are ready to handle them.

• Then, and only then, are they ready to present themselves to car salesmen as serious prospects.

• Finally, they go into the negotiating process determined to let the guys at the car store do the stewing. They know that those guys need us more than we need them.

For typical buyers, the serious shopping phase takes an average of about five weeks, from the time they start visiting car stores for test drives until the day they drive a new car home.

Following the smart buyers' lead, let's focus now on the car you drive today. We'll start with an illustration of what can happen when you don't keep a close eye on that ball.

Training is everything. The peach was once a bitter almond; cauliflower is nothing but cabbage with a college education.

> —Mark Twain

7

Divide

and

Conquer

Read the next paragraph twice.

Even if you're the world's worst price negotiator, the car store probably will make more profit selling your clean, well-maintained trade-in to someone else than it will make selling a new car or truck to you. *And that profit will come directly out of your pocket.*

It's a fact. Today the average dealer makes more profit selling used than new cars for two reasons: simple economics and simple new-car buyers.

THE SIMPLE ECONOMICS

New-car pricing is supercompetitive because every dealer has essentially the same merchandise to sell at the same price. A new Chevy Cavalier is the same car, with the same sticker price, at every Chevy store in town. In addition, new cars carry more overhead, from fancy showrooms to higher inventory financing costs. That makes it even more difficult to sell them for big profits.

By contrast, all used cars are different from one another, even when they're the same year, make and model. With no standardized sticker prices or dealer invoice costs and no easy way to measure their condition, especially that of the important parts under the hood, it's more difficult for consumers to evaluate their true worth. That makes it relatively easy for car stores to sell every one of them at a profit.

THE SIMPLE NEW-CAR BUYER

The key to a dealer's used-car profit is the new-car buyer. Two out of three deals include a trade-in. And most people literally give away their trade-in, without understanding what they really get for it.

That's because they don't watch all the balls. Instead, they let the salesman confuse the issue by juggling the new-car sell price and the old-car buy price in a single package deal.

They may think they're getting a great deal because the trade-in allowance is $1,000 over wholesale Kelley Blue Book or some other impressive-sounding measurement. They don't realize that the juggler's deal combines that apparently attractive trade-in allowance with a much higher new-car price than they could have negotiated without a trade-in. He's simply taking money out of one of their pockets and putting it in the other. By the time they agree to the package, it's all mumbo jumbo to them, but at least part of it sounds terrific.

The car store then turns their trade-in into a nice little money machine:

• If it's in relatively good shape and they need it in their used-car inventory, they'll spend a couple of hundred dollars making it look great and retail it themselves for a profit of $1,000 to $1,500 or more. (Two of every three vehicles taken in trade are retailed by the dealership; the average new-car dealer retails over thirty used cars every month.)

• If it's in relatively poor shape, or if they don't need it, they'll take a quick $300 to $700 profit by wholesaling it the next day to a used-car dealer. (In

1991, new-car dealerships wholesaled 5.4 million cars to other used-car dealers!)

Either way they'll probably make more money on that trade-in than on the new car they sold.

The bottom line is that customers with desirable used cars who buy this kind of trade-in allowance deal typically leave between $1,000 and $2,000 on the table.

If your car is an ugly hulk that barely wheezes onto the dealer's lot, you won't lose much by letting him take it off your hands. But if you have a clean, one-owner, average-miles-for-age vehicle that's mechanically sound, there are two ways to keep most of that money in your pocket:

• The best way is to *sell it yourself* at retail, as illustrated in Chapter 9.

• The second best way is to sell it to a dealer, but for its *true wholesale value,* as covered in the next chapter.

First, however, you must master the next rule. *It's the single most important factor to remember if you're going to succeed in this competition.*

DIVIDE AND CONQUER, COMBINE AND BE CONQUERED

The customers described here left a lot of money on the table because they let the salesman combine two elements that should never be combined: the selling price for the new vehicle and the buying price for their used vehicle. When they let him do that, they lost the ability to watch all the balls. As a result, they paid more for the new car than a smart buyer would have and received less for the old car than a smart seller would have. And they never knew either what they paid for one or what they got paid for the other.

Write this a hundred times on the blackboard of your mind:

> • **BUYING A NEW CAR IS ONE DEAL.**
> • **SELLING AN OLD CAR IS ANOTHER.**
> • **KEEP THEM SEPARATE AND YOU'LL WIN.**
> • **COMBINE THEM AND YOU'LL LOSE.**

Now let's develop the knowledge you need to keep them separate and thereby keep control of the negotiation.

8 The Wholesale Truth, and Nothing But

It's powerful pantomime.

The skilled salesman doesn't say a word as he checks out your trade-in. His hands do the talking, lingering over every little scratch or blemish—silently, but effectively reducing the vehicle's value . . . in your mind.

Don't attend this performance. Give him the keys and wait for his return. You'll have a punch line of your own: You'll know what it's worth.

The only right price for your trade-in is its actual wholesale value. Unless you know that number and make the salesman aware that you do, you will get less than true wholesale, and the car store will make an extra profit selling your old car. (You will never get more than true wholesale. If they offer more, the difference is coming from your wallet, not theirs, in the form of a higher price on the new car.)

Knowing your car's true wholesale value will also help you decide whether to trade it in or sell it yourself. You'll compare that value to the retail price you can expect to get from an individual, a subject covered in the next chapter. The difference will surprise you. If you decide to trade it despite this difference, at least you'll be doing it with your eyes open.

THE TRUTH ABOUT THOSE LITTLE BOOKS

How do you discover your car's true wholesale value? Not by looking in any book—blue, black or red—because those books don't reflect the current wholesale climate for your car in your market.

Remember, every used car is different, and local conditions always affect values. Yet one of those big-name little books actually admitted to us that the numbers are exactly the same in every regional edition it publishes! (Their numbers come primarily from auto auctions. Have you or your friends ever bought or sold a car at an auto auction?)

Those books will tell you whether your car is in the $10,000 or the $15,000 ball park, but they won't tell you reliably whether it's worth $9,700 or $11,200. And numbers for the same car can differ widely from book to book. (Be aware that many salesmen will pull out a lower-priced book when they're buying a used car and a higher-priced book when they're selling it.)

There's an old saying: Nobody has a decision to make until somebody makes them an offer. Well, those little used-car pricing books don't contain any offers, and you shouldn't use them to make any decisions. To get a number you can rely on, you need some real offers.

PLAYING THE GAME

You'll get those offers by playing a little game some afternoon, shopping your used car at some of the very stores near home or work where you'll eventually be negotiating for your new car. (We're assuming that you've got a vehicle that someone might find attractive, not a heap ready for the wrecking yard.)

First, make sure your vehicle is clean and mechanically sound. Then drive it to Automobile Row. Go to dealers selling the new vehicles you're interested in, but pull into their used-car departments and ask for the person who buys used cars. Get his name and write it down.

As he approaches, remind yourself that a relatively poor market for new-car sales is a good market for used-car sales, and that those conditions appear to be the new norm. Consumption-for-its-own-sake is out of fashion in the

'90s. Most people will be buying new vehicles because they have to, not simply because they want to. With fewer impulse buyers in the market and new-car prices climbing sky-high, it will take years for new-vehicle sales to recover to their mid-'80s levels of over 15 million a year. And with consumer confidence levels depressed by corporate restructurings and layoffs, more people will be opting for used cars instead of the more expensive new ones.

This is more than idle speculation: In 1990, franchised dealers sold more used than new cars for the first time since the end of World War II. It happened again in 1991, and the trend is expected to continue.

That means every used-car manager will continue to need good used cars. And with new-car sales down, there are fewer trade-ins of the attractive one-owner cars that are his bread and butter. He is very interested in buying cars like yours, no matter what he might say at first.

HERE'S THE SCRIPT

Tell him that you're planning to sell your car, you don't want the hassle of selling it yourself, you're visiting a few used-car dealers, and you'd like to know what he'd pay for it. (If he asks why you're not trading it for another, say you're buying your sister's year-old Chevy.)

He'll take the car, check it out and come back with a figure. Whatever number he gives, you should say nicely, "That sounds low to me. I got the impression from a couple of other dealers that it was worth more than that to a good used-car operation." *Then bite your tongue and wait for him to say something.*

If he says that's his final offer, you've learned what you came in for. Thank him for his time and drive to another store.

With most used-car managers, however, the first offer is typically a lowball opener to see how easy and uninformed you are. He might increase his initial offer right away. More likely he'll ask what the other guys offered, or what you want for it.

FOLLOW THE BOUNCING BALL . . .

Remember that your objective is to find out how much higher he might go, so that you can put a realistic wholesale value on your car. Your answer to his question will depend on the "value ball park" your car is in. Here are some rough guidelines for answers that will help you get to a realistic number:

- If his offer was under $3,000 but not wildly out of line as an opener for your car, tell him that based on what you've heard elsewhere you believe the car is worth *at least $500 more.*

- If his offer was between $3,000 and $5,000, tell him that based on other dealers' comments, you believe the car is worth *at least $750 more.*

- If his offer was between $5,000 and $7,000, tell him that based on what you've heard elsewhere, you believe the car is worth *at least $1,000 more.*

You get the idea. If your car's "value ball park" is higher than these examples, raise your response accordingly.

Most important, after you respond with a "bump," bite your tongue again! Don't say another word until he says something in return.

If he says your figure is way out of line, ask him if that means his first offer was his best offer. If he says your number is high, ask him how high he thinks it is.

Chances are, he'll counter with a better number than his opener. At this point, tell him (if it's true) that you're the only owner, you've got all the maintenance records, you just had the scheduled service done last month and all it needed was new brake pads. He's not going to have to invest big bucks in fixing anything.

Then pick a number halfway between your last figure and his, tell him you think it should be worth that much to him, *and bite your tongue again.*

At this point he might say it's not worth that much, that his last offer was his best one. Or he might agree with your new number and ask if you'd sell it to him for that price.

Your answer to either response should be, "I'll certainly consider it seriously. But first I'm going to make a few more stops. How long will your offer be good?" Make a quick note of the answer, tell him you'll get back to him in the next few days, thank him for his time and head for your next stop.

However the discussion ends, you've learned your car's true wholesale value to that used-car operation. Remember, however, that one used-car department might be fully stocked and not want your car unless they can "steal" it from you at a lowball price and wholesale it to a used-car dealer for a quick, easy profit.

To get a reliable estimate, you must repeat the same drill at a couple of other new-car dealerships (including at least one selling the make of your used car, where it would be a natural addition to their inventory) and at a couple of big used-car-only dealers. Be sure to ask each of them how long their offer will be good.

You'll spend half a day doing this, but it'll pay off—especially a week later, when a new-car salesman gives you a lowball trade-in offer for your car and you tell him that Joe Smith, *his used-car manager*, told you last week that he'd pay $1,000 more! And that's the wholesale truth.

Private individuals represent the majority of the used car market. They've sold over $57 billion in used cars annually without taking trades, providing warranties or service.

Right or wrong, buyers will pay more for a privately-owned car. Why? Trust.

—President of a consignment consulting firm that applies the real-estate sales concept to the used-car market (quoted in *Automotive News*, November 18, 1991)

9

Who Needs a Middleman?

The best way to avoid getting used by a new-car dealer is to avoid trading in a good used car. Instead, sell it yourself to an individual. It's more work, but it pays awfully well. The difference between wholesaling it to a car store and retailing it yourself can be $1,000 to $2,000 or more for a mid-priced car in good shape. (Generally, the better the condition, the bigger the spread between wholesale and retail.)

Why give that much money to a middleman, when there's bona fide demand for what you've got to sell?

Lots of people would rather buy a clean, well-maintained, one-owner car from an individual than take a chance on something from a used-car dealer. (In fact, 54 percent of used-car sales are between private parties.) These folks think they'll get a better car for less money. Also, they typically can get the historical maintenance records from the owner, and knowing how it's been treated gives them more confidence in its worth.

This preference may be strongest among *nonsmokers,* who now number seven out of ten U.S. adults. Many of them will even pay a premium for a nicotine-free vehicle!

To get a feel for retail prices of cars like yours, it's okay to start by calling your bank or credit union to ask what the used-car book says. *But remember, that book wasn't written about your car in your market this month.* You need to do more homework.

☎ REACHING OUT: LEARNING BY TALKING, NOT WALKING

Fortunately, you can do this homework on the phone. Check the ads in your weekend paper and in those used-car classifieds that seem to be everywhere. Call a few private sellers and ask about their cars—asking price, mileage, condition, equipment, type of driving done, and whether: (a) they're the original owner, (b) they've got the service records, (c) they've permitted smoking, and (d) the car has ever been in an accident. (Tell them you'd plan to have it checked by a mechanic who can tell.)

If it's a mid-priced car they're asking $6,000 or more for, find out how low they might really go by picking a number that's between $1,500 and $2,000 less and asking if they'd consider selling it for that price. If they refuse, bump the number in increments, starting with a couple of $500 bumps, followed by one or two $250 bumps until you find a price they'd consider. Thank them and say you'll think about it.

Then mentally compare your car with theirs to see if you think yours is worth more or less. If the cars are roughly comparable except that they're smokers and you're not, yours should be worth at least $300 more to a nonsmoking buyer, no matter what year or model.

Next, call a few new-car stores that sell your make and ask for their used-car department. Tell them that you're looking for a good, clean used car that's the year, make and model of the car you own.

• If they have one, ask about the mileage, how it's equipped, the asking price and (lastly) the color. If it's blue, tell them you want red or white and thank them. Don't give them your phone number.

- If they don't have one, tell them that you'd prefer to buy from a reputable dealer than from an unknown private party, and ask what would be a fair price. When they quote a price and say they'll find one, say you'll think about it, but you want to talk to a few more dealers. Thank them, but don't give them your phone number.

This exercise will give you a good idea of what your car is worth at retail, compared to other cars of the same year, make and model.

Based on this telephone research among private parties and used-car departments, you should be able to pick your expected price, the price you actually think you can get. Figure that this number is somewhere in the range between "realistic" dealer selling prices (probably 10 to 15 percent below their asking prices) and the prices those private parties would "consider." Then choose a *slightly higher* number for your asking price, keeping it below the used-car department's asking price.

Next, have your car detailed to make it look beautiful inside and out, have the oil changed and all the other fluids brought to the right levels, and fix any obvious engine, brake or wheel alignment problems that might shake a prospect's confidence during a test drive and kill a sale. Also make sure the radio, air conditioner, heater, defroster, lights, wipers and turn signals work.

NOW YOU'RE THE CAR SALESMAN

Now you're ready to call your newspaper and those used-car classifieds to place a weekend ad that describes the good things about your car. The hot buttons (if they're true) are one nonsmoking owner, low mileage, very clean, and complete service record. The service record can be particularly reassuring to many potential buyers, since many used-car swindlers buy high-mileage cars at auctions, roll back the odometers illegally and then pose as private parties selling "pampered, one-owner cars."

Don't put a price in the ad. Just say, "MUST SELL," and add the hot buttons just listed, your phone number, and the best weekday and weekend hours to call.

When they call and ask, give them that slightly higher asking price you picked, but make it clear that you've got some flexibility. If they ask for your rock-bottom number, tell them that you haven't established one. Say that some other people are interested in the car, that it's a one-owner car that's been reliable for you, that you're sure somebody is going to like it a lot, and that you're confident you'll be able to work out an agreeable price with that person. Then ask if they'd like directions to your place and about what time you should expect them.

If they like the car when they see it but make an offer that's well below your asking price, assume that's not their final offer. Counteroffer somewhere in between, but still above the price your research said you can expect to get.

To create a greater sense of urgency and value, try the old car salesman's trick: Say you've been offered $450 more by someone who's coming back in the morning. If they really want the car, chances are good they'll raise their offer when they hear that, and your excuse for taking it will be a bird in the hand.

If they like the car but instead of making an offer they ask what your rock-bottom number is, tell them you really don't want to sell the car for much less than your asking price, that you've done a lot of comparison shopping and know that's a fair price for a clean, one-owner vehicle like yours. Then counter by shaving a couple of hundred dollars off your asking price, but stay well above your expected price.

Always bite your tongue and let them react to your counteroffer before you say another word.

If they react negatively, ask them what they'd be willing to pay. If that's ridiculously low, reject it politely and thank them for coming, adding that it's clear they aren't that enthusiastic about the car and you're sure someone else will be. If their willing-to-pay number is not that bad but still below your expected price, counter with that price.

Somewhere in this kind of firm-but-flexible exchange, you'll get a price you'll find acceptable, one that's a lot better than any car store will give you.

A NOTE OF CAUTION

Unfortunately, we live in a hazardous world. One of the risks you face in selling your car yourself is that it could be *stolen* by a prospective "buyer" during a test drive. The thief may even leave another stolen car with you. (He may be trading up.)

Here are some thoughts on handling this potentially delicate situation:

• Don't let anyone test-drive your car unaccompanied.

• But be wary. You wouldn't get into a stranger's car alone, so why get into your car alone with a stranger? Have a friend accompany you.

• It's perfectly proper to ask a stranger for identification before permitting a test drive. Check a driver's license and a credit card, and leave those items with a friend or neighbor until you return. If the potential buyer carries no identification or won't cooperate, tell him that you're sorry but you won't allow anyone to test-drive your car without seeing and retaining proper identification.

• Trust your instincts. If you've got any reservations about a person, politely decline the request for a test drive.

• Some serious buyers will want to have your car checked over by a mechanic—an inspection they will pay for. That's a reasonable request, and a sign that you've got an excellent prospect. Again, however, you must be wary. You need a security deposit important enough to guarantee their return—perhaps a wallet full of important identification papers and credit cards; or their current car and keys, after checking the registration information against their other identification data.

Some prospects may be offended by your caution, but if you ask them to put themselves in your place most will say they'd handle the situation the same way.

TIE UP THE LOOSE ENDS NEATLY

In closing the deal, be sure to do these important things:

• Get a nonrefundable deposit in return for taking the car off the market.

• Ask the buyer to get a certified check made out to you for the full sales price and to meet you at your bank at a mutually convenient time to sign over the title. Don't give possession of the car until this is done.

• Write out a sales receipt, in duplicate, that says you've sold the car "as is" for the agreed amount, and include the buyer's name, address and driver's license number, plus the date and time of day and both signatures.

• Call your state's Department of Motor Vehicles to learn how to release your liability for parking and/or traffic violations and civil litigation resulting from operation after the date of sale. Obtain and complete the required form, and mail it promptly.

• Inform your auto insurance agent that you no longer own the car. He will advise you whether to transfer, suspend or cancel your coverage.

We haven't tried to touch every base in this sell-it-yourself lesson. We've focused primarily on the money issues. If you have questions and need more counsel, you should call the financial institution that has your auto loan, your auto insurance agent, your state's motor vehicle department or your local auto club for more information.

Now let's look at the issue of financing. (If you're paying cash, you can skip to Chapter 11.)

Let us all be happy and live within our means, even if we have to borrow the money to do it.

—Artemus Ward

10

Auto Financing 101

Always remember that everything that happens in a car store is designed to make money for that store. There's nothing wrong with that; it's our free enterprise system at work. And that same great system can work for you, too, if you take action at every step to keep it competitive. The first step is shopping for money, and the time to do it is before you visit any car stores.

DON'T GET REAR-ENDED

When you get down to negotiating a final deal, the salesman is going to want you to "buy" your financing money through his store. As indicated in Chapter 5, that's an important source of his store's profit on the back end of the transaction.

That's when another interested party will get involved—the F&I (finance and insurance) manager. There is a lot of pressure on him to add profit to every deal. He usually gets a commission on anything you buy on the back end, including financing and the life and disability insurance he'll try to include in the transaction. (Some F&I managers make more money than any salesman in the store.)

The dealership may arrange financing through a bank or finance company, or through the auto manufacturer's captive finance operation. These captives, such as Ford Motor Credit or General Motors Acceptance Corporation, are very important sources of credit. They provide about 40 percent of all new-car financing, roughly the same percentage accounted for by banks. The captives typically handle between 30 and 60 percent of the financing for their own vehicles. (GMAC is the largest finance company in the country, with more than $100 billion in assets.)

Understand, though, that no matter which company does the actual financing, the car store acts as a middleman and receives a commission or fee for its service. Most often, this income comes from a dealer finance reserve, which is the difference between the contract rate charged to the consumer and the retention rate earned by the bank or finance company.

As a rule of thumb, figure that a car store can *double* its gross profit on a sale if it arranges the financing. No wonder there's pressure there!

Depending on the deal with the lending institution, the car store's participation fee can amount to 5 percent or more of the loan. The longer the term and the higher the rate, the more interest you pay . . . and the more commission the car store receives.

Let's assume the dealer "buys" the money for an average-size auto loan of $14,000 from a lending institution at 8.5 percent interest and "sells" it to you on a 48-month loan at 10.5 percent interest. Over a four-year period that little 2 percent spread will put a $645 profit in the dealer's pocket, nearly 5 percent of the loan amount.

SURPRISE: THE DEALER'S DEAL MAY BE A GOOD ONE

You may find that the financing available through the dealership is quite attractive. These days auto manufacturers are offering subsidized, lower-interest financing plans through their own finance companies to stimulate sales.

Some manufacturers also have "first-time buyer" financing programs to start building brand loyalty among a younger audience. The rates are typically higher than standard bank rates, but these programs are often geared to people who might not qualify for standard bank auto loans simply because they have little or no credit history.

So whether it's your first car or your twenty-first, the car store's current financing options are *always* worth checking out. *But doesn't common sense say that you should be able to buy money cheaper if there's no middleman's commission for the financing entity to pay?*

The only way to know whether the financing options the dealership presents are attractive is to shop competitively for money before you sit down in a negotiating session at any car store. Then, when you're in that session, you'll be able to compare the annualized percentage rates (APRs) charged under the different alternatives.

Unfortunately, many new-car buyers don't even bother to check out their financing options before entering the F&I manager's den. The Consumer Bankers Association reports that about 80 percent of a bank's new-auto loans are originated indirectly, at dealerships, whereas only 20 percent result from buyers visiting the bank themselves to prequalify for a loan before they purchase a vehicle.

As a result, every year hundreds of thousands of car buyers who could have qualified for direct auto loans at lower rates end up paying a lot more money *to the same banks,* with the difference going to the car stores. Welcome to America, folks—the land where the average consumer is more interested in the convenience of one-stop shopping than in smart money management. Fortunately, you are not going to fall into that trap.

SHOPPING FOR MONEY: A PRIMER

As a first step, you should decide the highest monthly payment you can handle comfortably, *including auto insurance.* Call your insurance agent and tell him what vehicles you're considering. He'll be glad to tell you what your insurance will cost. (He works on commission, too.) He may even influence your final choice if you find that one alternative costs much less to insure than another.

Then decide on a down payment. If part or all of this will come from the sale of your current car, go through the steps in Chapters 8 and 9 to learn what it's really worth under each of those scenarios.

CAUTION: DON'T DRIVE "UPSIDE DOWN"

As a general rule, we'd advise putting at least 20 percent down on any new vehicle and financing it over a maximum term of four years. If you can't handle those numbers without changing your lifestyle dramatically, you should buy a less expensive car. This advice may sound conservative, but it will help keep you from getting "upside down" when you want to sell or trade again.

You're "upside down" when the actual value of the vehicle is less than the principal you still owe on the loan. You've got negative equity in the car, and you'd literally have to pay someone to take it off your hands. Here's why it's easy to get "upside down" whenever you combine a small down payment with a long financing term (such as 10 percent down and a six-year loan):

• New cars are *terrible* investments. Knowledgeable people will tell you that, depending on the specific vehicle and the timing of your purchase, *most new cars or trucks depreciate from 15–20 percent to as much as 35–40 percent in the first few weeks you own them!* Only the most prestigious high-end luxury cars seem to hold their value significantly longer.

• Add the fact that your monthly payments will include more interest than principal until you get into the latter part of the payment schedule, and you can see how a car's value can go down much faster than your equity in it goes up.

After you've decided whether to follow our 20 percent down/four-year rule or some other payment program, you're ready to contact some banks, your credit union and other new-car financing sources. (If you belong to a credit union, you should start there. Credit union rates on auto loans are typically at least one percent lower than bank rates. One reason: Credit unions usually don't provide a participation fee to car stores.)

☎ REACHING OUT AGAIN

Start this process on the telephone by calling a loan officer about car loans. Say that you're starting to shop for a new vehicle, that you want to line up financing first, that your credit report is clean, and that you'd like some help in finding the "price ball park" you should be shopping in. (We'll assume in the illustration below that you're following our 20 percent down, four-year guideline.)

First ask for their annualized percentage rates (APRs) on car loans. They will typically be higher for lower down payments and, sometimes, for longer payment schedules.

Tell the loan officer that you'd like to learn how large a loan you can afford if you put 20 percent down and finance a car over four years. Then take the total monthly payment you decided on, subtract one sixth of the semiannual auto insurance premium, and ask how large a four-year loan you could pay off with the remainder.

Add to that loan amount the down payment you decided on previously, and you'll have *the maximum price* you can afford to pay under those terms. (Remember, that total must cover state and local sales taxes, license and title fees, and any other up-front costs. Since license fees can be substantial, you should call your state's licensing agency and ask them to estimate the fee for a car in your price range.) Then, consider whether it's reasonable to expect to buy one or more of the vehicles you're interested in for that price or less, given what you'll learn in Chapter 15 about what they cost the dealer.

If your maximum affordable price is a lot lower than the dealer's invoice cost, and there's no current consumer rebate offer or factory-to-dealer incentive program, the answer is probably no. That means you've got to lower your sights to a less expensive vehicle, find more down-payment money, or ignore the 20 percent down/four-year rule and risk getting "upside down."

HERE'S SOMETHING THAT MIGHT HELP

Before you make that call, use the amortization table below to determine what the monthly payment would be for a given three-, four- or five-year loan.

As you can see, we've chosen annual percentage rates from 7.5 to 14, which should cover most of the realistic range. The dollar amounts in the table are the monthly payments per $1,000 borrowed. For example, assume you're borrowing $13,500 for four years at an annual percentage rate of 10.5. To calculate your monthly payment, go to the 10.5 percent column and find the payment per thousand for a four-year loan, $25.61. Multiplying that number by 13.5 (the number of thousands you're borrowing) gives you the monthly payment—$345.74.

Payment Factors Per $1,000	Annual Percentage Rates						
	7.5%	8.0%	8.5%	9.0%	9.5%	10.0%	10.5%
3-year loan	31.11	31.34	31.57	31.80	32.04	32.27	32.51
4-year loan	24.18	24.42	24.65	24.89	25.13	25.37	25.61
5-year loan	20.04	20.28	20.52	20.76	21.01	21.25	21.50
	11.0%	11.5%	12.0%	12.5%	13.0%	13.5%	14.0%
3-year loan	32.74	32.98	33.22	33.46	33.70	33.94	34.18
4-year loan	25.85	26.09	26.34	26.58	26.83	27.08	27.33
5-year loan	21.75	22.00	22.25	22.50	22.76	23.01	23.27

MAKING THEM COMPETE

You should shop for a money deal as aggressively as you're going to shop for that auto deal. Financial institutions are in a competitive business, too. (They only "book" about two thirds of the auto loans they approve.) Let them know you're shopping their competitors, and you'll borrow where you get the best terms.

It's worth the extra effort. According to the 1992 Automobile Finance Study collected by the Consumer Bankers Association, the average new-car loan in 1991 was over $13,000. That's a lot of money for most people to pay off in four years. If you could drop the interest rate on that average-size loan just one percent by shopping competitively, you'd save about $300 in interest payments.

If your local bank quotes a rate higher than a bank five miles away, tell the loan officer you'd prefer to do business in your neighborhood but their rate is higher. Ask if that's absolutely the best they can do. She or he may have to get approval from another manager, but banks are in business to sell money and you may find there's room to negotiate. It's also common for a bank to give a slightly lower rate if you have an account there and the monthly payment is deducted automatically.

You can do a lot of comparison shopping on the telephone. In many cities you can even arrange your loan by telephone, calling in your application and getting an answer within a day or two.

Frequently, however, in-person meetings are advisable when you get down to two or three loan finalists, especially if you sense anything less than an enthusiastic response on the phone. Financial institutions want to build relationships with successful people, and being well-groomed and well-dressed can help create the right climate for loan approval.

Here are two more tips on financing.

1. Explore "the non-auto auto loan"

You may find, as *Fortune* suggested in its 1992 Investor's Guide, that "a home equity credit line is a cheap, tax-smart way to buy a new car." That's because interest is tax-deductible on home equity borrowings up to $100,000, whereas other personal loan interest (including interest on standard auto loans) is not. The Consumer Bankers Association reports that nearly 11 percent of home equity loans are used to finance autos.

Home equity loans and lines of credit come in many forms, with either fixed or variable interest rates, and with and without "origination points." In most cases, you'll probably pay a lower *effective rate* than you would for a regular car loan, simply because the interest is deductible.

For example, if you're in the 31 percent tax bracket and the loan's annual percentage rate is 10.5, your net effective rate after taxes is only 7.25 percent. That may be significantly lower than any standard car loan rate you're likely to find. (We're not CPAs. You should check with your tax advisor for the best counsel.)

Incidentally, you will find *Money* magazine's monthly charts of "Leading Loans in the Largest Metro Areas" a useful source of information for both auto and home equity loans, with phone numbers to call for more information.

Another side to this that you should keep in mind is that with this type of financing, you'll be pledging *your home* as collateral. If there's any reason to be nervous about your ability to make those payments, you might sleep better with a standard auto loan, knowing that all they can repossess is your car, not your roof.

You should also note that Congress has become alarmed by a decline in the equity held by homeowners, caused in part by a sharp rise in tax-deductible home equity loans used for vacations and auto purchases. The lawmakers asked the General Accounting Office to investigate equity borrowing. After receiving the GAO's report, Congress may move to curb these tax advantages.

This makes it mandatory that you check with the appropriate tax counselor before proceeding.

2. Beware of the credit insurance rip-off

Don't get pressured into buying credit life insurance as an add-on. You'll often find this item buried in the mouse type in your auto loan documents. These policies are very profitable to both the insurance companies and the sellers—financial institutions and auto dealers, who can earn commissions of 30 to 50 percent.

Money magazine reported that these policies pay out an average of only 38¢ in benefits for every dollar of premium, compared with 83¢ for the typical life insurance policy! And a spokesperson for the National Association of Insurance Commissioners has urged consumers to be particularly cautious of an insurer recommended by a *lender*, who is "going to be looking for the product with the highest commission, and that's usually the company that charges the highest premium."

By law, the purchase of credit life insurance cannot be a precondition for receiving a loan. Yet many people buy it. In 1991, Ford Motor Credit Corporation reported that of the automobiles financed through a dealership, half of Ford's customers buy credit life insurance and 30 percent buy accident and health (disability) insurance. It's reasonable to project similar numbers to the other major auto manufacturers' captive credit operations.

If you feel you need any type of extra insurance coverage, discuss it with the agents you or your friends and relatives already deal with, and chances are you'll save a lot of money. Standard life and disability insurance policies are generally much better buys.

The bottom line: If you follow the steps we've suggested in this brief financing lesson, you'll be in a good position to determine whether the financing available at the car store is an attractive alternative for you or just a good deal for them.

11

The Fine Art
of Shopping
Without Buying

In the spring of 1991, a postal worker took his 1990 car to a dealership in Providence, Rhode Island, for an oil change. To kill time while he was waiting, he browsed the showroom, admiring a fancy new sports car. Three salesmen converged on him.

Within minutes he found himself in the credit manager's office, loudly proclaiming that he wasn't in the market for anything new except oil. Before he knew it, he owned that sports car and a five-year payment schedule totaling $40,000.

He sued the dealership for engaging in deceptive trade practices. According to the Associated Press, his lawyer said, "I don't think he actually realized any paperwork had gone through. They made [him] feel empowered and enthusiastic about purchasing a new car. But the fact is [the dealership] took him for a ride and left him financially stranded."

W hile you're working on determining what your car is worth, deciding whether to sell it at wholesale or retail and getting your financial ducks in a row, you should also get to know some new cars well enough to narrow your choices to two or three finalists. You've been salivating over new-car ads for months. You know which models seem most appealing. Maybe you attended the annual automobile show when it came to town. You've studied the December new-car issue of *Kiplinger's Personal Finance Magazine,* the *Consumer Reports* April auto review issue, and other sources for safety, economy, reliability and insurance cost ratings.

Even with all this information, narrowing your choices may not be easy. According to *Automotive News,* domestic and foreign manufacturers offered 555 passenger car models for sale in the United States in the 1992 model year! And there won't be any reduction in the next decade.

The real challenge, however, isn't the number of cars; it's the number of car salesmen. You need a safe and secure way to get through the test-driving and information-gathering stage without getting caught up in the juggler's act. Here's how to accomplish that and live to tell about it.

First review Psychology 101 in Chapter 4 (pp. 14–15), especially the part about projecting total emotional detachment. Then play the little game outlined next.

MAKE THIS AN AWAY GAME, IF YOU CAN

If you live in an area that has several dealers for each major make, gather your information at car stores that are relatively farther from your home or office. That way, when you're ready to start serious negotiations with stores closer to home or work, you'll be an unknown quantity, without the implied commitments of previous visits. (The less a salesman knows about you, the less money he'll get from you.)

That doesn't necessarily mean you should ignore those more distant stores in your final negotiations. Indeed, you may drive a better bargain with them because they'll see you as business they normally wouldn't get. They may agree to a lower gross deal just because you're an out-of-town bird in hand. But, as you'll learn in Chapter 20, there are real advantages to buying your new car from a dealer who's more convenient, ideally the one who'll service it regularly.

Plan these trips by checking the dealer association's advertising in your newspaper, where you'll probably find the names and addresses of all the dealers for a given make in your metropolitan area. You may even find a map showing their relative locations. (Dealers love to put maps in their ads!)

Choose the stores you'll visit, grab a pen and a pad to take detailed notes, *leave your checkbook and your credit cards at home,* and jump in your car.

Your objective on this trip is to narrow your choices to a few specific cars that will meet your requirements and make you a happy driver for the next several years. Smile, this is going to be fun!

THE GAME PLAN

As you enter the showroom, walk briskly to one of the younger-looking, less experienced salesmen. Tell him you're just starting to look at new cars, and yes, you do plan to buy one soon. But no, you're not a candidate to buy one today under any circumstances. There are several makes you want to research and test-drive before making a decision.

You have no idea what you'll end up buying. It'll depend on a lot of (unspecified) things. But he's got a couple of cars that are on your list, and you'd like to test-drive them, learn about their features and benefits, and get some literature to review at home.

While you're in this tire-kicking stage, test-drive at least two different cars you like at each dealership. Make those test drives long enough to put the cars through most of the paces you'll require of them every day. And be sure to drive cars equipped the way you think you'll buy them. (Don't test an automatic transmission if you want a stick shift or the four-door sedan if you want the coupe.)

Even if you love both cars, try not to show it. Remember that your behavior should say, A car is a car. I'm going to check them all out and buy the best deal.

When you're around that salesman, act undecided, uncommitted, even a little wishy-washy. For each car, comment on things you like and things you don't like. (If you like everything, invent a few things you don't like.) That will keep him from moving into his aggressive selling posture with the "if" questions designed to get verbal commitments, such as "If I got you the right price, would you buy this car today?" When he asks that, your correct answer is, "Not today. As I told you, I'm just starting to narrow my choices. I've got more appointments to test-drive cars today and tomorrow, and I plan to keep them."

ANYTHING YOU SAY WILL BE USED AGAINST YOU

Remember, the one who asks the questions controls the conversation. So ask him all the things you need to know, such as "What rustproofing warranty comes with the car?" And "What specific direct consumer incentives is the factory offering this month on the cars you sell?" And one he probably won't answer in detail, "What specific factory-to-dealer cash incentives are in effect this month?"

But when he asks you questions, your stock answers should be, "I don't know," "I'm not sure," "I need to discuss it with my spouse," and "I'll have to think about that." When those get tired, answer a question with a question—for example, "How do most people answer that?"

In this little game, you'll get the information you need, but he'll get nothing concrete to move toward his objective of closing you before you leave. (Remember, he's in a sell-it-now-or-never business, but you're in a don't-buy-it-now mode.)

After test-driving cars you particularly like, write down the key information from the *manufacturer's* window sticker (not the dealer's separate sticker): the vehicle identification number, model number and suggested retail price for the base car, plus the contents and prices of the optional factory equipment packages and other accessories.

Then thank the salesman for his time. Take his card, but don't give him your phone number or address. If he discovers that you live two gas stops from his store, he'll decide that it's now or never and try to chain you to a chair until you buy.

Above all, don't get roped into his office to talk about anything, including the weather. He's going to want you to sit down for a minute "just to see what it looks like on paper." Tell him politely that you're not ready to do that, and that you've got appointments to test-drive three other makes. Both statements will be true.

If you live in a smaller market without many dealers for the same make, you can't play the game exactly like this. But the essential rule still applies: *You want to get all the information you need while giving him none of the information he needs.*

NARROW THE FIELD, BUT NOT TOO MUCH

After a day or two, you should be able to narrow your choices to a few favorites. Try to keep at least two or three in the running. The big winners in this game will be those who maintain several options right down to the finish line. A single choice isn't an option, it's an obsession—one that's potentially very expensive.

SHAKE THE FAMILY TREE

One good way to open options is to consider "family relations," vehicles that have different brand names but are made by the same manufacturer and are quite similar. The key differences often will be in trim levels, but there also can be meaningful price differences.

For example, Chrysler's highly praised new mid-size sedans, the 1993 Dodge Intrepid, Eagle Vision and Chrysler Concorde, were sisters, with prices starting at $15,930, $17,387 and $18,341, respectively. The range in base prices was over $2,400.

At any time, there could also be hefty manufacturer incentives offered on some family members but not on others.

If you like one branch of a family tree you may like another almost as well. And pricing and incentive differences may be meaningful enough to swing your choice to a vehicle you hadn't considered at the start.

Here is a list of 1993 "family relations," some of which are the products of joint ventures between automotive manufacturers (e.g., Ford and Mazda):

"FAMILY RELATIONS"—1993 MODEL YEAR

General Motors

- Buick Century & Oldsmobile Cutlass Ciera/Cruiser
- Buick LeSabre, Oldsmobile Eighty-Eight Royale & Pontiac Bonneville
- Buick Park Avenue & Oldsmobile Ninety-Eight
- Buick Regal, Chevrolet Lumina, Oldsmobile Cutlass Supreme & Pontiac Grand Prix
- Buick Roadmaster & Chevrolet Caprice
- Buick Skylark, Oldsmobile Achieva & Pontiac Grand Am
- Cadillac De Ville & Cadillac Sixty Special
- Cadillac Seville (4-door) and Cadillac Eldorado (2-door)
- Chevrolet Astro & GMC Safari
- Chevrolet Beretta (2-door) & Chevrolet Corsica (4-door)
- Chevrolet Blazer & GMC Yukon
- Chevrolet S10 Blazer, GMC Jimmy & Oldsmobile Bravada
- Chevrolet Camaro & Pontiac Firebird
- Chevrolet Cavalier & Pontiac Sunbird
- Chevrolet Lumina APV, Oldsmobile Silhouette & Pontiac Trans Sport minivans
- Chevrolet S10 pickup & GMC Sonoma pickup

- Chevrolet full-size pickups & GMC Sierra pickups
- Chevrolet Sportvan & GMC Rally
- Chevrolet Suburban & GMC Suburban

Chrysler (and Partner Mitsubishi)

- Chrysler Concorde, Dodge Intrepid & Eagle Vision (new mid-size sedans)
- Chrysler Imperial & Chrysler New Yorker Fifth Avenue
- Chrysler LeBaron Sedan, Dodge Spirit & Plymouth Acclaim
- Chrysler New Yorker Sedan & Dodge Dynasty
- Dodge Caravan & Plymouth Voyager minivans
- Dodge Colt, Plymouth Colt, Eagle Summit & Mitsubishi Mirage
- Dodge Grand Caravan, Chrysler Town & Country & Plymouth Grand Voyager minivans
- Dodge Shadow & Plymouth Sundance
- Dodge Stealth & Mitsubishi 3000GT
- Eagle Summit wagon, Plymouth Colt Vista & Mitsubishi Expo LRV
- Eagle Talon, Mitsubishi Eclipse & Plymouth Laser

Ford (and Partners Mazda & Nissan)

- Ford Crown Victoria & Mercury Grand Marquis
- Ford Escort, Mercury Tracer & Mazda Protegé/323
- Ford Explorer & Mazda Navajo (2-door only)
- Ford Probe & Mazda MX-6
- Ford Taurus & Mercury Sable
- Ford Tempo & Mercury Topaz
- Ford Thunderbird & Mercury Cougar
- Mercury Villager & Nissan Quest minivans

Others

- Geo Metro & Suzuki Swift
- Geo Prizm & Toyota Corolla
- Geo Storm & Isuzu Impulse
- Geo Tracker & Suzuki Sidekick
- Hyundai Excel & Mitsubishi Precis
- Toyota Camry V6 XLE & Lexus ES 300

THE SMART SHOPPER'S TIEBREAKER

If you're having difficulty choosing a favorite, here's an idea that beats flipping a coin: Consider *renting* each finalist for a day or so on weekends, as a way to learn more than you can in those brief test drives. This will set you back a few dollars, but the rental cost pales in comparison to the $17,000 mistake of buying the wrong car.

You may have to make several calls to find what you want, but most popular domestic and import models can be rented. In fact, many dealers rent cars by the day.

However you narrow the field, remember to retain one or two fallback choices. At this stage, throwing away alternatives is throwing away leverage.

There's one more factor to consider that could have a big financial impact if you make the wrong choice. It's a by-product of the intensely competitive U.S. auto market, and most people never give it a thought. You'll find several thoughts on it in the next chapter.

12

Here Today.
Here
Tomorrow?

Following a decade that attracted new auto makers to the United States, the 1990s will be the decade when some companies pack their bags and go home.

—Maryann Keller,
automotive analyst and
Managing Director–
Research, Furman Selz,
Inc., New York
(quoted in the
Los Angeles Times,
August 30, 1991)

FACTS

• In the first seven months of 1991, 2,240 customers bought a new Peugeot automobile and 1,878 bought a new Sterling. Then, in early August, both Peugeot and Sterling announced they would quit selling cars in the U.S. market after their modest existing inventories were depleted.

• In 1991, 8,963 people bought a new Daihatsu car or truck. Then, early in 1992, Daihatsu announced it would withdraw from the U.S. market at the end of the 1992 model year.

- In 1991, 3,092 customers bought a new Yugo, and in the first quarter of 1992, 1,412 people made the same decision. Then, in April 1992, as civil war was destroying the country where the vehicle was produced, Yugo announced it was bankrupt and unable to continue doing business in the United States.

QUESTIONS

- Aren't you glad you're not one of those 17,585 people who bought a new Peugeot or Sterling or Daihatsu or Yugo in 1991 or 1992 before those farewell announcements were made?
- How many buyers would have made a different decision if they had known what was coming?

The "Disappearing Car Company" factor is a by-product of the intensely competitive U.S. auto market in the 1990s. Most shoppers never give it a thought, but it could have a big financial impact if you make the wrong choice.

Why? Because it raises questions about the cost and convenient availability of parts and service for those vehicles, including basic warranty service.

More important, it raises those questions among potential second owners. And the lingering doubts could reduce the resale value of those vehicles significantly. Even if the dealer body remains intact and reassures buyers that they'll always be there, the questions won't go away.

Why take the chance that this might happen to you, especially when you can virtually guarantee that it won't, if you make a safe choice.

LIMITING YOUR RISK

You know that the biggest companies won't go away. Their financial fortunes will ebb and flow, but General Motors and Ford and Toyota/Lexus and Honda/Acura and Nissan/Infiniti are going to be here at the end of the decade. So is Chrysler, despite the speculation you may have read about the company needing a partner to operate successfully beyond the late 1990s. (In mid-1991, it was reported that Ford "kicked Chrysler's tires, but walked away.")

It looks like Lee Iacocca's last hurrah at Chrysler will result in another impressive business turnaround. Following an aggressive cost-cutting program, Chrysler's production efficiency now approaches that of the Japanese. The company dominates the profitable minivan market and has introduced some impressive new products that should improve its position in other key segments. The Jeep Grand Cherokee has been a big success. And the mid-size LH sedans—the Chrysler Concorde, Dodge Intrepid and Eagle Vision—are expected to become strong bread-and-butter entries that will finally make Chrysler a real contender as a car company.

Chrysler has announced that it will combine the Jeep-Eagle and Chrysler-Plymouth divisions by the end of the decade. As part of this consolidation, the company considered eliminating the Eagle and Plymouth brands. But consumer research showed that each filled an important consumer niche, and Chrysler decided to keep them in its long-term product plan.

Following the board-led upheaval that shook stodgy, money-losing General Motors to its roots in 1992, the new management team is moving aggressively to return the company to profitability. Its key job: allocating resources most effectively. One question they're examining is why the company needs so many models that essentially duplicate each other under different names.

Although GM may simplify its product lineup by pruning weaker models and reducing the number of overlapping offerings, it has strongly affirmed to its dealers and the public that it does not plan to eliminate any brands. And you can count on being able to get parts and service for any discontinued models through GM franchises.

WE'RE NOT FORTUNE-TELLERS, BUT...

Beyond these Big Six companies, which account for about 90 percent of the market, the crystal ball gets cloudy. In our opinion, one or more of the other import makes will decide to follow Peugeot, Sterling, Daihatsu and Yugo, leaving this market before the decade ends.

The U.S. automobile market will remain intensely competitive. The cost of entry is huge. But the real killer is the cost of continuing to play—developing and marketing new product every four to six years, when the price tag for an all-new model is a cool $1 billion. The Big Six have the resources to do it; many of the others don't, except as long-term smaller fry with specific expertise at filling certain niches.

The stronger niche players—Mazda (25 percent owned by Ford), Mitsubishi, BMW and Mercedes-Benz—undoubtedly will survive here.

• Both Mazda and Mitsubishi are solid second-tier companies with strong dealer networks. To move toward tier-one status, we believe each needs a high-volume (100,000+/year) mid-size sedan to compete with the Honda Accord, Ford Taurus and Toyota Camry. But with or without it, they're here to stay. (It's worth noting, however, that in October 1992, Mazda abruptly canceled plans to launch its Amati luxury-car division in the spring of 1994.)

• BMW's sales dropped from almost 97,000 in 1986 to under 54,000 in 1991. But with the new 3-series reversing the decline and a plan to start building cars in South Carolina in 1995, BMW promises to be a serious competitor in the luxury/performance segment well past the year 2000. As the president of BMW of North America has said, "To sell 65,000 cars in the U.S. is nothing. You're not going to be a strong player in the long run if you just hang around this figure."

• Mercedes-Benz suffered a similar sales decline, from over 99,000 in 1986 to under 59,000 in 1991. But new products and aggressive marketing underscore Mercedes' commitment to the U.S. market. With world-class engineering, timeless styling and a heritage to match, the Mercedes brand name will be an unassailable asset here as long as affluent people drive cars.

Saab and Jaguar have become relatively marginal, lower-volume entries, but they're owned by GM (50 percent of Saab) and Ford (100 percent of Jaguar), and international corporate pride will keep them around.

• Saab's sales in the United States dropped from over 48,000 in 1986 to about 26,000 in 1991. GM has seen a lot of red ink from this 1989 joint venture investment. It has poured $1.5 billion into Saab and must inject more capital in 1993 to enable Saab to continue operating.

• Jaguar sold over 24,000 cars here in 1986, but less than 10,000 in 1991. Ford acquired Jaguar for $3.1 billion in 1989 and has been losing money ever since. In July 1992, Jaguar's chairman said the company needed to sell over 35,000 cars a year worldwide to break even, but he expected to produce only about 28,000 in 1992.

These brands may not survive here as separate, stand-alone franchises. By the end of the decade you may see them only in multi-make dealerships, with names such as John Smith Oldsmobile-Saab or Millville Ford-Jaguar.

There are other companies, however—those without real niche

strength or owners with deep pockets—that will find it increasingly more difficult to compete here successfully.

The cost of advertising alone is a long-term problem for some. We estimate that the threshold expenditure required to maintain strong brand awareness today is about $100 million a year. Ford, GM and Chrysler together spend $2.5 to $3 billion, averaging around $300 per vehicle. By contrast, a third-tier importer selling 100,000 cars yearly would spend $1,000 per vehicle at that threshold advertising level.

With Ford and Chrysler nearing parity with Japanese production costs, it's issues like advertising clout that keep some import-make managers awake nights. Inevitably, we believe, a few of them will decide to throw in the towel.

THE MORE SERIOUS THREAT: THE "DISAPPEARING DEALER" FACTOR

Even if all the relatively weaker companies continue to sell their autos here, there's another aspect to weakness that every car shopper should consider before taking the final plunge. Call it the "Disappearing Dealer" factor.

A long-term sales decline doesn't necessarily mean that an automobile *company* will go away. But there's a real risk that many of its *dealers* will go away, as they find they can't make a living selling that make. They (and their banks) own a multimillion-dollar sales and service facility, and if the old make no longer supports that investment, they'll find a new make that will.

The erosion of a weakening make's dealer body is not a subject you'll read about in the newspaper or hear about on TV. That's because there's a quiet gentlemen's agreement not to run stories unfavorable to auto companies or dealers—an agreement that's effectively enforced by more than 8 billion automotive advertising dollars.

But that erosion exists, and it could impact thousands of auto buyers. Here are some sobering facts about several smaller makes:

• Volkswagen sold over 217,000 vehicles in the United States in 1986, averaging 20 per month per dealer. But 1991 sales were under 92,000 (only 11 per month per dealer), marking the first time since 1958 that VW sold fewer than 100,000 cars here. And VW's sales were down another 22 percent in the first ten months of 1992. One consequence of lower sales: Volkswagen's dealer base shrank from 914 in January 1987 to 688 in

November 1992. Volkswagen is a very successful company in Europe, where its market share exceeds 17 percent, but it has become a distant also-ran among imports in this market.

• Porsche sold over 30,000 cars here in 1986, almost 8 per month per dealer. But sales were only about 4,400 in 1991, less than 2 per month per dealer. And Porsche's dealer count dropped by a third, from 322 to 218; 40 dealers departed in 1991 alone.

• Subaru's U.S. sales dropped from over 183,000 in 1986 (19 per month per dealer) to only 105,000 in 1991 (12 per month per dealer). Over that period 79 dealers left the franchise, though the exodus has stopped in recent years. Subaru's U.S. president resigned in August 1992, saying he wasn't enjoying his job (probably an understatement). And Subaru's parent company, Fuji Heavy Industries, is counting on boosting sales quickly to 130,000 a year, "the minimum units [needed] to keep a sales network in the whole United States." That will be a tough assignment, given Subaru's current product line and its apparently limited ability to fund the big-time marketing activity required.

• Audi, owned by Volkswagen, sold about 74,000 cars here in 1985, then got roasted on *60 Minutes* in 1986 over an unproven charge of "unintended acceleration." It's been on the critical list ever since. Sales in 1991: 12,283, only 3 per month per dealer. As a result, the dealer base dropped from 408 in January 1986 to 309 in July 1992.

What if your dealer had been one of these dropouts, and the nearest surviving dealer was two counties or two freeways away? In terms of the cost and convenient availability of parts and service, wouldn't the impact on you have been the same as if the company had withdrawn from the U.S. market?

Actually, losing a dealer might even be worse than losing a company. If the company leaves, but your dealer has another strong franchise in a dual operation, he'll probably continue to service the departed make in the same facility.* But if your dealer gives up the company's franchise, you're left dependent on the nearest surviving dealer for parts and service.

Here's a quick look at some other import makes with significant sales declines in recent years.

---

*That's what has happened with almost all Peugeot, Sterling and Daihatsu dealers. Yugo owners face a more bleak future. There is no surviving entity to honor Yugo's warranty obligations or to handle any emission or safety recalls. There may not even be a reliable source of spare parts for the over 141,000 Yugos sold in the United States since 1985.

- Hyundai went from over 264,000 sales in 1988 to under 118,000 in 1991. Despite that drop its dealer base mushroomed from 277 to 495. And its Korean parent, one of the largest industrial companies in the world, seems committed to this market. Hyundai's biggest hurdle: overcoming its reputation for making cars of relatively poor quality.

- Isuzu lost over $400 million in 1991, selling under 100,000 trucks here for the first time since 1984. In late 1992 the company announced it would "suspend development of passenger cars" and concentrate on trucks, recreational vehicles and diesel engines. General Motors owns almost 40 percent of this affiliate, but given all its other problems GM is not in a position to make massive additional investments to prop up this sagging brand. Despite its sales decline Isuzu is not losing dealers; it had 600 in July 1992—about 260 more than in January 1987.

- Even once-invulnerable Volvo bears watching. As competitors have added airbags and other protective features, Volvo seems to have lost its exclusive ownership of the safety image. With little fresh-looking product, Volvo's sales dropped about 40 percent, from over 113,000 in 1986 (23 per month per dealer) to under 68,000 in 1991 (14 per month per dealer). Its dealer base has remained stable at about 400, but if sales keep slipping we believe their loyalties will be tested.

The signs are not good. Volvo has the capacity to build 350,000 units a year, but produced only 204,000 1992 models. In September 1992, the president of Volvo's U.S. operation announced his resignation just as officials in Sweden were announcing further cost-cutting measures they hoped would make Volvo profitable again by 1995. *The Wall Street Journal* quoted a company newsletter in which the Swedish president said, "The situation has worsened since summer. Quite simply, we have to sell more cars at somewhat higher prices." That may not be possible if economic conditions—and demand for Volvos—don't improve dramatically in Sweden, other European countries and the United States.

We can't predict which companies will have real staying power in this market. But the purpose of the game is to make a profit, and that's become an elusive goal for even the largest players in recent years.

There are simply too many automotive companies, with too much production capacity, trying to sell too many different vehicles through too many dealers to too few prospects. If one third of all the companies, cars and dealers disappeared overnight, consumers would still have a cornucopia of choices.

This is the perfect recipe for a continuing buyers' market and more red ink for the manufacturers. It won't change until the "too manys" come into balance with the "too fews." But with so much corporate pride at stake in the world's largest industry, you can bet it'll take a lot more bad news to convince the weaker entries to leave this market.

We think that bad news will arrive. It seems only a matter of time before a few more import makes decide they're in over their heads, pack their airbags and leave.

The moral of this story: *The potential cost of a Disappearing Car Company—or a Disappearing Dealer—is a hidden item on the price sticker of every declining, loss-plagued import make.*

Review Chapter 3 (The Big Picture). As you decide which makes to consider, keep your eye on the business pages. If one or more of your favorites seem to be losing sales and money, and it's becoming a habit, maybe you should cross them off your prospect list.

Forewarned is forearmed, right? We can't give you the answer, but we'd be remiss if we didn't raise the question.

13

Saturn:

A Different

Kind of Deal

Now, they finally have a car do what GM said it would do—compete on a quality basis with small Japanese cars, specifically the Honda Civic—and the most creative thing they can come up with is a no-haggle pricing policy that, while supposedly for the benefit of the consumer, is really just another price hike in disguise.

—From a consumer's letter written in response to an August 17, 1992, cover story on Saturn (printed in *Business Week,* September 14, 1992)

The folksy, down-home ad campaign for GM's Saturn subsidiary carries the tag line, "A Different Kind of Company. A Different Kind of Car." They could add, "A Different Kind of Deal."

There's apparently a lot to like in Saturn, General Motors' version of a Japanese subcompact. It's earned the third-highest customer satisfaction rating in the J. D. Power and Associates Initial Quality Study^{sm}; only Lexus and Infiniti scored higher. *Car and Driver* called it "the luxury econocar, tightly built and brimming with niceties."

Designed as an import fighter, it's doing its job well; about half of Saturn's customers would have opted for an import instead. And seven out of ten sales have been to people who would not otherwise have bought a GM product.

But the biggest difference between Saturn and the rest of the auto industry isn't in the car, it's in the deal. *There isn't any.* If you want a Saturn, you'll pay the full sticker price, even if the sales manager is your brother-in-law. The reason: *There's no competition between dealers for your business. And there isn't going to be any.*

THE KEY: ELIMINATING COMPETITIVE GEOGRAPHY

Starting with a clean sheet of paper, Saturn was able to give each dealer a large exclusive sales territory. Each market area will have only one retail "owner," which effectively eliminates price competition between Saturn dealers. This exclusive selling territory could be one part of a huge market, like Los Angeles, or the entire metropolitan area of a smaller market, such as Grand Rapids.

There were 182 Saturn stores on July 1, 1992. Eventually, the number will reach about 800, with 250 to 300 dealers each owning from two to four stores in their designated marketing areas.

With no other Saturn dealers within a reasonable shopping radius, you won't be able to play one dealer off against another to negotiate price. Although GM will say that a dealership may charge what it wishes, the cold, hard fact is that the sticker price is the real price. *Think of it as a legal form of retail price-fixing.*

It's also Saturn's policy not to offer rebates or other incentives—which saves GM anywhere from $500 to $1,500 per vehicle, depending on the competitive climate.

The bottom line for consumers: They are going to pay more for a Saturn than they would if Saturn had been, say, just another Chevrolet model instead of a new, separate GM division with an exclusive-territory dealer network.

The bottom line for dealers: They are going to make a lot more money under this exclusive-territory pricing umbrella. With front-end gross profits per sale ranging from $1,100 to $1,700, we'd guess Saturn is the most profitable small-car franchise by a country mile.

HAVING THEIR CAKE AND EATING IT: A PSYCHOLOGICAL COUP

Fixed pricing doesn't seem to hurt sales: In the first half of 1992, Saturn sold more new vehicles per dealer than any other auto franchise, including Toyota (which sells both cars and trucks). Dealers are selling every car the factory can make, and many have waiting lists of buyers.

Ironically, Saturn's "no-dicker sticker" is a key ingredient in its success because it eliminates the haggling over price. In the showroom, for a refreshing change, Saturn customers are treated like a bona fide form of intelligent life. The salespeople simply help them fall in love with the car, tell them that the sticker price is fair and (most important) assure them no one will get the car for less. No sales pressure is applied.

In grateful response, Saturn buyers pay more than they would for comparable small cars sold by dealers willing to negotiate and factories willing to use rebates. They're so focused on the new-and-improved purchase process that they actually enjoy paying more. And, we believe, the halo of this more pleasant shopping experience carries over to enhance their ratings of the vehicle itself. (Isn't a diner more likely to praise the food when the chef has been a superb host?)

And most don't have a clue that the dealer's profit on their purchase is much greater than he could realize with any other small-car franchise in America.

The financial picture isn't nearly as rosy for General Motors. They've invested about $5 billion in Saturn, and it's not clear when their stockholders will see an adequate return on that investment. Small cars don't produce big profits per unit. Saturn's production capacity is limited, and the capital infusions requested by other needy GM divisions may represent more critical corporate priorities than expanding Saturn.

In this climate, the prognosis for a Saturn prospect is "more of the same": More demand for limited production. Perhaps more aggressive price increases than for other domestic cars. And no deals for anyone.

WHAT'S A SHOPPER TO DO?

You've got two choices:

1. *If your heart's set on a Saturn, relax and enjoy it; it's a great little car, and you're striking a blow for U.S. economic resurgence.* Instead of haggling over price, you'll be treated like visiting royalty. And why shouldn't you be? You're paying the sticker price!

(Think about it for ten seconds. If you called any dealer in the United States and told him you were on your way down to pay the sticker price for one of his cars, he'd probably send a chauffeur-driven limousine to pick you up. At that price, you'd have a wonderful sales experience anywhere.)

The Saturn dealer might make twice the profit on your purchase that he's making selling more expensive cars in his non-Saturn stores. But you'll have the consolation of knowing that the next customer will make a similar contribution to his welfare. No one will walk in and get the car you bought for $1,000 less. It seems almost un-American, doesn't it?

Here's choice number two:

2. *If Saturn is only one of your finalists, you should shop the competition aggressively.* (Broadly, that includes the Mazda 323 and Protegé, Toyota Corolla and Geo Prizm, Ford Escort and Mercury Tracer, Nissan Sentra, Honda Civic, Toyota Tercel, Plymouth Sundance and Dodge Shadow, among others.) You may like some better than Saturn, and you shouldn't have to pay the sticker price for any of them.

Facing more flexible dealers and frequent factory incentive programs, you may even discover you can afford a higher trim level in another car for the price of Saturn's lower-level offering. As one reader wrote in response to *Car and Driver*'s comparison of sub-$10,000 cars, "Except for the Saturn, all the cars in your comparison could be purchased in Southern California for about $8,000, including sound system and air conditioning. Only Saturn dealers refuse to dicker. The real competitors in the Saturn's price range are the four-door upscale models of the cars you tested. Saturn offers good value, but in the real world it is not necessarily the best buy."

Saturn is a different kind of company. Exclusive sales areas are a terrific idea for both the company and its dealers. But if all automotive franchises were set up that way, U.S. consumers would spend billions of dollars more on basic transportation every year.

14

One-Price, "No-Dicker" Dealers: Oasis or Mirage?

It's a marketing gimmick that dealers use, just like red tag sales, Labor Day sales, you name it. And if you say it's going to sweep the nation and it's going to be all one-price dealerships, you're crazy. It's not going to happen. It's simply not going to last.

—Executive vice president of the Greater Los Angeles Motor Car Dealers Association, in an article on the emergence of one-price, "no-dicker" dealers (from an Associated Press release printed in *The Long Beach Press-Telegram*, September 21, 1992)

By late 1991, before the initial sales year ended, it had become clear to the automotive establishment that Saturn's greatest achievement was getting American car buyers to pay the sticker price for every car, and that the key to pulling off this startling coup was the elimination of haggling over price. Success in any field breeds imitation.

THE SATURN WANNABES

Other dealers, watching Saturn's apparently magical scenario unfold, decided to play follow-the-leader. They had seen the new religion, and they were converting—dumping their high-pressure sales forces and becoming one-price, "no-dicker" dealers.

That "fair" price would be somewhere between the sticker price and the dealer invoice price. It would be noted on a separate "civilized sticker" placed on each car, and there would be no bargaining. What you see is what you pay. For everyone.

At present, there are probably a few hundred "no-dicker" dealers in the country, a tiny fraction of the 22,000+ franchised dealerships. Some of them made the switch in desperation; sales were so poor, they had nothing to lose. Others simply thought it was a good idea and wanted to reap the benefits of getting there first in their markets.

Their problem: They don't have Saturn's fail-safe formula working for them. (It's like grafting an eagle's wings onto a pigeon; that pigeon can soar, but without talons it can't catch fish.)

Let's examine how this pricing transplant works, from both consumer and dealer perspectives.

FOR THE SHOPPER, THERE'S LESS THERE THAN MEETS THE EYE

How do these "no-dicker" dealers operate, from the buyer's perspective? In the spring of 1992, J. D. Power and Associates conducted a study of twenty-four dealerships that had adopted the system relatively early. The findings, widely reported by the Associated Press, revealed the following:

1. *"No-Dicker" dealers make more profit.* (Otherwise, why do it?) Nine out of ten dealers reported increased sales since adopting the program. And half the dealers said their average gross profit per car had gone up; the other half split equally between those whose profits were the same and those with lower profits per sale.

Overall, the "no-dicker" system seemed to be doing what it was designed to do: get the consumer to pay more for new vehicles.

2. *Today's price is just that; tomorrow's price is anybody's guess.* If consumers expect to have a Saturn-like experience at other "no-dicker" dealers, leaving confident that no one will buy the same car for a lower price next week, or tomorrow, they're in for a surprise.

- The research showed that 33 percent of these dealers changed their "civilized" prices as factory incentive programs changed (a frequent occurrence).

- Another 29 percent of the dealers changed prices as their inventory conditions changed (another frequent occurrence).

- And 14 percent of dealers changed prices "when they needed to boost volume," another 14 percent changed them weekly, and 10 percent changed them every two or three days!

So buyers may have a more enjoyable shopping experience, but they will pay more for the car, and someone else may pay a lot less for the same vehicle tomorrow. And in most cases, they'll still have to dicker over their trade-in allowance and deal with the F&I manager on financing and back-end options.

Does that sound like what you expected, or hoped for, when you heard about one-price, "no-dicker" dealers? (We don't think so.)

FOR THE DEALER, "NO-DICKER" IS NO NIRVANA

Without the Saturn-like umbrella of exclusive sales territories, "no-dicker" dealers are trying to light a match in a deluge. Here's why we don't think you're going to see this selling policy adopted broadly:

- In most large markets there are several dealers for the same make. (Chevrolet, for example, has about 4,500 dealers nationally.) When one adopts a "no-dicker" policy, he becomes a sitting duck for the others, who can cut prices selectively, on request, to steal his customers.

- The 80/20 Rule of Life still applies. Many dealers will be reluctant to give up their shot at the least knowledgeable 20 percent of the buyers, the ones who probably provide 80 percent of the profits.

- In effect, one-price selling says to the customer, "Pay it or go somewhere else." That's not a message most dealers want to deliver. They'd rather make a small profit than lose the sale to a competitor.

- "No-dicker" is a better strategy for tough times, when sales are hardest to come by. As consumer confidence improves and sales traffic increases, and as long-term supply conditions come into better balance with demand, "no-dicker" will make less economic sense to dealers.

As a spokesperson for the National Automobile Dealers Association said in response to questions about the "no-dicker" movement, "Dealers sell the way they do because it works. They are real wizards at local marketing, and they do what works."

• Finally, and most important, the bulk of dealers can't change to "no-dicker" successfully unless the customer changes, too. But the customer has been trained under the current system, the one dealers use "because it works."

What are the chances of most shoppers buying a car at the first price offered? Slim, indeed. After decades of 20,000 dealers shouting "shop us last" in their advertising, the cumulative impact has taught consumers that there will always be a better price down the street.

As a former mega-dealer in Los Angeles said before he closed his last store, "People will shop you silly, and they should, too . . . sooner or later, someone will sell you a car for the price you want."

The retail auto dealers of America forced the customer's genie out of the bottle a long time ago, and they can't put him back with "no-dicker" stickers. Until the other automotive franchises find a way to reinvent their distribution channels, providing exclusive sales territories for a smaller number of dealers, Saturn will be the only make that can enforce this policy consistently. And when the supply of Saturns catches up with demand, we'd bet even those dealers will be hard-pressed to avoid dickering.

Long-term, the market is going to set the price. Supply and demand: it's the law.

FOR SMART SHOPPERS, THE "NO-DICKER" DEALER IS A USEFUL TOOL

Use him! If the "no-dicker" price is friendly enough, buy from him. If it's not, use it as a place to start negotiating with other dealers. To win your business, they'll have to beat it, maybe by a lot.

DON'T CONFUSE A FACTORY'S "ONE-PRICE" OFFERINGS WITH "NO-DICKER" DEALERS

There's another, related movement afoot, one with real consumer benefits. Led by Ford, manufacturers have begun to package certain models with a standard list of popular options and offer them for an attractively low price. In some cases, they may sell all versions of the vehicle at the same price.

• For 1993, Ford reduced its number of Thunderbird models from four to two, added an impressive array of options and cut prices dramatically. The Thunderbird LX went to $16,292 from $20,316 for the 1992 model, a slightly more loaded car.

• Ford's 1993 Escort was offered with power steering, air conditioning and other goodies for $10,899—hatchback, sedan and wagon.

• Honda announced it would offer a "value" version of its Accord in the spring of 1993.

The manufacturers and their dealers would like to sell these cars on a "no-dicker" basis. But it's not unusual to find them offering rebates on these one-price cars. As Ford's general manager said, "We can suggest a price, but if the market won't bring it, the dealers are going to cut into their gross to make the deal."

These specially equipped and priced vehicles can be great buys. And if you shop around, you're likely to find some price flexibility, too.

It happened at the 1992 National Automobile Dealers Association convention in Dallas. The president of Chevrolet's Dealer Council got up and asked his cohorts to sell one more Chevy a week, even if they made no profit on it.

Why? Because that would mean another 250,000 Chevys sold each year, giving loss-plagued GM billions more for badly needed new-product programs over the next five years. (And you thought those guys had no heart.)

The lesson: Learn what those cars really cost the dealer. Because, yes, you can buy them for cost, or very close to it.

15

Learn the Cost or Pay the Price

The centerpiece of your ability to negotiate effectively will be your knowledge of what that car or truck is going to cost the dealer. That, of course, is the last thing the dealer wants you to know. He wants his salesmen to negotiate based on the sticker price, not the cost.

IT'S A THREE-PIECE PUZZLE

Three key elements determine the dealer cost of any vehicle:

1. Dealer Invoice Price—the actual factory invoice billed to the dealer.

2. Factory-to-Dealer Incentives—cash paid only to dealers, details of which are not widely publicized to consumers.

3. Dealer Holdback—a portion of the factory invoice price which is collected and held back by the manufacturer, then refunded periodically to the dealer as the vehicles are sold. Holdback has been used for decades by General Motors, Ford and Chrysler. In the last few years, several imports have adopted the concept. Today holdback applies to eight of every ten vehicles sold in the United States.

Without learning about all three elements, you can't get a good fix on what the dealer pays for a given vehicle. Let's tackle them one at a time.

THE STARTING POINT: DEALER INVOICE PRICE

This is the actual price billed by the factory, the invoice the dealer must pay when the vehicle is delivered to his lot. (Typically, the dealer pays the manufacturer with money he borrows under his "flooring plan" credit arrangement with a bank or finance company or with the auto manufacturer's finance subsidiary. He pays the lender interest until the car is sold, then repays the loan.)

To determine this figure, you need a printout of dealer invoice prices for the specific vehicle or vehicles you're considering. To get familiar with the kind of information contained on a printout, turn to pages 170 and 171 of the Appendix and look at the simplified pricing data we've created for a fictitious car and manufacturer—the 1993 All-American Speedster, built by the All-American Motor Corporation. And as you review the information for this imaginary vehicle, keep in mind that you may order complete, current pricing data for the actual vehicle you're interested in directly from us. See Chapter 25 for details.

Our simplified printout for the All-American Speedster contains the following information:

• You will find both the Dealer Invoice Price and the Manufacturer's Suggested Retail Price (MSRP), which is the price you'll see on the sticker attached to the window of each new car or truck. Note that the list shows pricing for all available bodystyles and trim levels, from the least expensive "low end" Speedster model to the most expensive "high end" model.

• Just below the initial price table you will find a complete listing of all the standard equipment items that are included in the base price of each trim level.

• You will then see dealer invoice and retail price information for all available factory-installed optional equipment and accessories, including those sold as packages and groups.

• The Factory Code column on the far left carries the actual manufacturer's computer code, the number by which each model or accessory is ordered or identified, just as it appears on the window sticker of a new car or truck.

It's important to have a printout covering all the configurations a manufacturer offers for a given vehicle. Without the complete picture, you can't make price/value comparisons between different trim levels. (For example, a higher trim level frequently represents a better value because it includes standard equipment in the base price that would be treated as extra-cost options in a lower trim level.)

Building Your Worksheet

Once you have the current pricing printouts for the vehicles you're interested in, you can determine the dealer invoice cost for the specific models you want, outfitted with the exact optional accessories and equipment you choose. To illustrate how easy this is, we'll build a simple worksheet using the pricing data we've created for our fictitious car—the 1993 All-American Speedster.

• Let's assume you're interested in a Speedster wagon. You don't want the lowest trim level (A), but you can't justify spending an extra $3,000+ for the highest trim level (AAA) because you really don't need things like luxury cloth upholstery and a tachometer. So you settle on the middle trim level (AA, Factory Code S87), with a sticker price of $15,200 and a dealer invoice price of $13,000. Note that we have entered these numbers on the New-Vehicle Worksheet on page 73.

• Looking at the Preferred Equipment Packages available for the AA wagon, you're attracted by Factory Code 444B, which includes air conditioning, rear window defroster, AM/FM stereo radio w/cassette, power door locks, power windows and cruise control. The package price is less than what the items would cost separately. The retail price is $1,800; the dealer invoice price, $1,500. We have added these numbers to the worksheet on page 73.

• You'd also like to have a more powerful engine than the standard 3.0-liter V6. Looking at the Equipment and Accessories list, you see that you can add a 3.8-liter V6 (Factory Code 947). Sticker price: $560; invoice: $470. These numbers are also placed on the worksheet.

• The only other item you want is a rear-facing third seat (Factory Code 314). This adds $130 invoice, $160 retail to our worksheet.

• We must also add the $500 destination (freight) charge. Note that there is no markup on freight; the dealer simply charges the buyer what the manufacturer charges him. Note also that the sticker price does not include sales taxes or license and title fees.

• Adding the subtotals in the two columns, we find that there's a difference of $2,620 between the suggested retail price ($18,220) and the dealer invoice price ($15,600). This difference is a starting point for understanding the dealer's real cost, but it's not the whole story, as the last few lines of the worksheet imply. We'll return to those lines later in this chapter.

We'll discuss in Chapter 21 exactly how to use this dealer invoice cost information in the negotiation process. For now, let's just say that the $2,620 difference between the dealer's cost and the retail price allows significant room for price movement, in your direction.

Pricing Credentials You Can Count On

At some point in the shopping process, a salesman is likely to tell you that your information on dealer invoice pricing is wrong. If you received your pricing data from us, you may confidently invite him to take out the vehicle's actual invoice for a comparison.

The reason you can be confident in the numbers is at the bottom of every page you'll receive, where it will say "Copyright by H. M. Gousha, a division of Simon & Schuster." H. M. Gousha has been publishing *The New Car Cost Guide* since 1956. This is the original pricing guide for new cars, and it has set the standard for timely, accurate, reliable and complete data.

Gousha's *New Car Cost Guide* is used by loan officers in financial institutions, car rental and leasing companies, fleet administrators, insurance adjusters, purchasing agents and other automotive professionals. These people must have accurate pricing data to do their jobs. And both the

NEW-VEHICLE WORKSHEET

Factory Code #	Model & Optional Equipment	Dealer Invoice Price	Suggested Retail Price
S87	**1993 All-American Speedster AA 4-Door Wagon**	$13,000	$15,200
444B	**Preferred Equipment Package** (air conditioner, rear window defroster, power door locks, power driver seat, power windows, cruise control, AM/FM/cassette, P205/65R15 SBR blackwall tires)	1,500	1,800
947	**3.8-liter V6 engine upgrade**	470	560
314	**Rear-facing third seat**	130	160
	Subtotals	15,100	17,720
	Plus Destination Charges	500	500
	Subtotals	15,600	18,220
	Less: **Direct Consumer Rebate** (coming up next)	750	
	Less: **Factory-to-Dealer Incentives** (also coming up next)	200	
	Less: **Dealer Holdback** (to be discussed after that)	532	
	Subtotals	14,118	18,220
	Less: Assumed **Year-End Carryover Allowance** (After 1994 models are introduced. Covered in Chapter 16.)	886	
	Grand Totals	$13,232	$18,220

vehicle manufacturers and their franchised dealers have a vested interest in the ability of these people to do their jobs.

We are a licensee of H. M. Gousha. They keep our pricing data current with regular computer updates.

The Monroney Doctrine

That sticker on the window of every new car is known in car-store jargon as the Monroney, after Oklahoma's Democratic Senator A. S. ("Mike")

Monroney, the lawmaker who sponsored the 1958 bill that mandated its presence. (Be sure to refer to it as "the Monroney" early in your negotiations, and the salesman will know he's not dealing with someone who just fell off a turnip truck.)

Monroney's federal law requires that label to include the make, model and identification number of the vehicle; the suggested retail price of the auto and all factory-installed options not included in the base price; and the amount charged to the dealer for delivery to his store.

It's a federal crime to remove or alter that sticker before the vehicle is delivered to the ultimate purchaser. This effectively prevents car stores from replacing the original with a higher-priced sticker if a manufacturer raises the price on subsequent shipments of the same vehicle.

Truck Buyers, Beware

Unfortunately, there's one gaping loophole in the law: It doesn't apply to pickup trucks, which represent about one sixth of the automobile market. In the vast majority of cases, you will find the Monroney label on pickup trucks. But you may run into a few car stores that have replaced the original stickers on some. Manufacturers frequently increase prices during the model year, and some dealers may take advantage of this loophole to change the stickers on their trucks to the latest price, regardless of when they were purchased.

How can you detect this sticker exchange? In a couple of ways. First, look for the EPA label, which contains the federally mandated fuel economy information. This labeling almost always appears on the lower portion of the Monroney sticker, but it may appear legally as a separate label. If a pickup truck's mileage estimates (City MPG and Highway MPG) are on a separate label, there's a chance that the other sticker, with the pricing information, has been changed.

If you have doubts, compare the sticker formats on the new cars on the lot with those on the new trucks. If they differ considerably, that's another indication they may have replaced the Monroneys with their stickers.

How should you deal with suspected sticker switchers? *Our advice would be not to deal with them at all, unless they come clean.* Ask to see the original Monroney. Check the VIN number (vehicle identification number) against the one on the car. It's at the base of the front windshield, on top of the dashboard on the driver's side, where the police can find it easily. If they won't cooperate, find a car store with nothing to hide. There will be plenty of them.

In addition to the invoice price, two other factors influence the dealer's real cost. We'll now look at one of them—factory-to-dealer incentives.

THE INCENTIVES GAME

When Chrysler hired Joe Garagiola more than a decade ago to stand up on TV and say, "Buy a car, get a check," it changed the fundamentals of new-car marketing forever. Enticing buyers with direct cash rebates opened a Pandora's box that no one can close.

You'll read periodically that "manufacturers have decided to raise prices by cutting incentives." The number of incentive dollars spent per vehicle tends to rise and fall somewhat with changing market conditions. But as one industry analyst put it, "Incentive programs are like hard drugs; once you get on, it's hard to get off." The consumer has been trained to expect incentives, and fierce competitive pressure will keep them around as long as there's excess production capacity.

U.S. manufacturers spend an estimated $1,000+ per vehicle on incentives. (For example, Chrysler's incentive costs averaged $1,250 for each vehicle sold in the second quarter of 1992.) Even the Japanese, immune from the "incentive disease" for years, now spend an estimated average of $500+ per vehicle, with the second- and third-tier companies spending relatively more than Toyota or Honda.

Who's paying for this? You, the car buyer, of course. That extra $500 to $1,000+ is simply built into the price of every car sold. That means that the only way to get your money's worth is to buy a car that carries an incentive. Buying one that's not "incentivized" is like making a $500 to $1,000+ contribution to the manufacturer, who will give it to another buyer.

But wait, there's more to this incentive game than just a check in the mail from Joe Garagiola!

The Other Side of the Incentive Coin

Did you ever sit in front of late-night TV and wonder how so many dealers can shout about "prices below dealer invoice," implying that they're selling them for less than they paid? What they're trying to do, in dealer jargon, is "create a sense of urgency" that will get us off our couches and into their showrooms. The best way to do that, apparently, is to convince us that they're almost giving those things away.

But how can dealers sell cars and trucks for less than they cost? The answer, of course, is that they can't. At least they can't for long and stay in business, and who wants to buy a car from a dealer who's about to go out of business?

So, when they spend all those ad dollars implying that's what they're doing, are they telling us less than the whole truth or even misleading us? The answer lies somewhere between yes and no. Yes, because a dealer can sell cars all day long for less than he paid for them and still make money. And no, he can't sell cars for less than they cost him without losing money.

What He Paid for It Is Not What It Costs

Yes, the dealer invoice cost is what he paid for the car. It's the bill he got from the manufacturer, the invoice he had to pay when the auto arrived. But what he paid for the car is not what it ends up costing him because there are several ways manufacturers put money back into his pocket— money that's directly related to the sale of that specific vehicle. One of the ways they do this is through factory-to-dealer incentive programs.

Manufacturers are putting big bucks into these programs. These dollars to dealers can range from $200 up to $2,000 or more per sale on mid-priced vehicles, depending on how badly they want to move the vehicles. (The incentives can get as high as $10,000 on slow-moving luxury cars.)

There's just one problem: Nobody's telling you, the customer, about most of these incentives, yet you're the one who's ultimately paying for them.

The Mushroom Treatment

Since they don't publicize the details of these programs, we're kept in the dark, like mushrooms. All we hear are those commercials telling us to "come on down to take advantage of those [unspecified] factory-to-dealer incentives." There's a good business reason they don't tell us more. And realistically, if you ran a car store, you wouldn't want consumers to know the details, either.

Although this factory money is tied to the sale of a specific vehicle, a dealer may use it for any purpose he wishes. He may pass it along to the customer in the form of a lower price, but that will seldom be his first choice. He'd rather use it to motivate his salesmen, increase his advertising, upgrade his service bays or even paint the building. Most of all, he'd like to pocket it as extra profit, just as you would if you owned a car store.

Here's what the president of one of the world's largest automobile companies had to say on the subject: "A dealer typically says, 'Give me the money, I know how best to use it.' In principle, they always say that. In principle, they're right. But let's face it, [when] we give the money to the customer, it all goes to the customer. Give the money to the dealer, and some of it ends up in the profit of the dealership."

For example, one import manufacturer gave dealers the option of taking incentive money of $1,000 per sale either as dealer cash or as customer rebates. According to the company's national sales manager, only 15 to 20 percent of the dealers opted for the customer rebates. What a surprise!

With factory-to-dealer cash incentives, it's a case of what you don't know can't hurt the car store. Why give those factory dollars to people who don't ask for them? And how can we ask if we don't know they exist? As *The Wall Street Journal* reported in a March 8, 1991 article on one manufacturer's dealer discounts, "As in the past, the money will be paid to dealers instead of consumers, and [the factory] won't publicize the discounts. So buyers will have to bargain for the money, and many might not know the discounts are available."

Believe it or not, some dealers don't tell their own salesmen about these incentives! That's because they want to retain control over how the money is used. That makes good business sense for them, but car buyers are the ones paying the bill. And knowing the details can help them negotiate better.

CarDeals to the Rescue

On pages 172–182 of the Appendix, you'll find a detailed list of both the factory-to-customer and factory-to-dealer incentive programs that were in effect on August 7, 1992—just as the 1992 model year was winding down. This four-page report, called *CarDeals,* is updated every two weeks. The information is compiled from "reliable industry sources" by the Center for the Study of Services (CSS), a nonprofit consumer service organization in Washington, D.C. Here's what *CarDeals* covers:

Direct-to-Consumer Offers

Although it's relatively easy to learn about factory-to-customer incentive offers, whether they're cash rebates or below-market financing plans, *CarDeals* includes the current details as part of its one-stop incentive information service. In the listing, these customer offers are the ones followed by a "C."

Direct consumer offers are typically either a specific cash rebate amount, or a choice between a cash rebate and a factory-subsidized reduced-rate financing plan, all of which are detailed in the listing. Frequently, you're going to have to decide whether the rebate or the financing plan is better for you. The answer will depend on the size of the rebate, the annual percentage rate (APR) of the factory financing plan, the APRs available from other lenders, the amount you'll be borrowing and the length of the loan.

On pages 183–184 of the Appendix, you'll find a table that will help you compare rebates with financing plans. It was prepared by William Bryan, director of the Bureau of Economic and Business Research at the University of Illinois at Urbana-Champaign. The table lists a range of possible market interest rates down the left side and a range of factory-subsidized rates across the top. It covers loan terms from two to five years. The dollar numbers represent savings per $1,000 of loan amount.

To illustrate how to use this table, let's assume that you were shopping for a 1992 Ford Taurus in August 1992, when this issue of *CarDeals* was current. According to the information on the seventh page of *CarDeals* (page 178 of the Appendix), in the Midsize Cars section, a buyer of a 1992 Taurus had the choice of either a $750 to $1,000 cash rebate (depending on the region of the country he or she lived in) or Finance Plan 4, a 7.9 percent APR for up to 48 months (finance plans are detailed on page 182).

Which is more valuable—the rebate or the financing offer? Assume you thought you could buy the Taurus you wanted for about $16,500, including all taxes, title and license fees. You plan to make a 20 percent down payment of $3,300 and borrow the remaining $13,200, paying it off over four years (the maximum term we recommend). Your bank has quoted a 10 percent APR, and the factory plan's rate is 7.9 percent.

The table shows that with a factory-subsidized rate of 8 percent (the closest number to 7.9 percent), you'd save $37.44 per thousand dollars borrowed, or $494.21 over four years (13.2 × $37.44). Since this is less than the $750 rebate, you'd accept the customer cash alternative. As a general rule, rebates of $750 or more usually turn out to be more attractive than the financing alternatives for cars costing under $20,000.

To help us complete our worksheet on the fictitious 1993 Speedster wagon on page 73, we've assumed that the All-American Motor Corporation is making the same offer and entered a $750 rebate on the appropriate line.

Important note on sales taxes: Some "how to buy a car" books advise having any rebate credited as a discount in the selling price, as a way to avoid paying sales tax on the amount covered by the rebate. Unfortunately, that advice usually won't work. Most states tax the full sales price before the rebate (and, often, before any trade-in allowance is subtracted). Check your state's tax laws.

Incidentally, some states base the tax on the amended net sales price, after deducting any trade-in allowance. (In theory, you've already paid the tax on the trade-in.) Although this may save you a few hundred dollars in taxes on the new vehicle, you're still likely to come out ahead by selling your current car yourself at retail, instead of trading it in at wholesale.

Direct-to-Dealer Offers

Now let's look at the money manufacturers pay dealers to sell cars to you. These harder-to-uncover dealer incentives are followed by a "D" in the *CarDeals* listing. As you review these programs, the Center for the Study of Services suggests that you keep the following points in mind:

• *Some of these programs pay dealers more money per car as they sell more cars during the program period.* Unless otherwise noted, when you see a range in the listing (for example, the $800 to $1,600 range shown for 1991 and 1992 Isuzu Q16 pickup trucks on page 180 of the Appendix), this means that a dealer gets more cash per car if he sells more cars.

• *In some programs, all dealers have the same volume targets.* That means you can expect larger dealers to get bigger cash payments than smaller dealers, simply because they'll sell more cars. Everything else being equal, you should be able to negotiate a better deal with a large dealer during these programs.

• *In other programs, large dealers must meet higher volume targets than small dealers to qualify for incentive cash,* so there's no reason to expect a better deal at a large dealership.

• To help you differentiate these program types, the *CarDeals* listing tells you which ones are based on sales targets set for each dealer, as opposed to targets that are the same for all dealers. For example, see the generous 1992 Nissan Stanza program shown in the Compact Cars section on page 176 of the Appendix. Dealers received from $1,500 to $2,000 per car, based on individual sales targets. If a dealer met those targets by September 2, the end of the promotion period, he got cash for all Stanzas sold in the period.

• Returning to our pricing worksheet on the fictitious 1993 Speedster wagon on page 73, let's assume that All-American Motor Corporation's dealers can earn factory cash up to an extra $200 per vehicle, based on individual sales targets. You'll note that we've added that $200 to the Factory-to-Dealer Incentives line on the chart.

We'll discuss in Chapter 21 exactly how to use this dealer incentive information to your advantage during the negotiating process, along with the previously outlined dealer invoice cost data. For now, let's just say that since you're the one who ultimately pays for it, you're entitled to at least part of the benefit, and there's bound to be a dealer or two who'll want to sell you a car badly enough to agree.

Living Proof: Vehicle Options Can Be Valuable

With a current issue of *CarDeals,* you can examine the listing to see whether any of your finalist vehicles are covered by incentive programs. That's when you may discover a very tangible benefit of keeping more than one car on your list. It's not unusual at any time for the maker of one car to be offering a consumer and/or dealer incentive of $500 to $1,000 or more, while the maker of a similar car offers less, or none at all. That difference may be just what it takes to make one car the best choice for you.

To illustrate, let's assume that in August 1992 you were interested in a top-of-the-line 1992 Mitsubishi Eclipse GSX—the one with the 16-valve, turbocharged engine and full-time all-wheel drive. Turn to pages 181 and 182 of the Appendix. You'll see in the Sporty Cars section that there was a factory-to-dealer cash offer on the Eclipse ranging from zero to $1,200, depending on the number sold by September 30.

But the virtually identical four-wheel-drive models of the Eclipse's sister cars, the Eagle Talon and the Plymouth Laser, offered direct customer rebates of $1,500 each. In addition, they carried sticker prices that were $2,429 and $2,966 below that of the Eclipse GSX. Knowing all that, you might have found them to be very appealing alternatives.

If you've got your heart set on just one vehicle, and it isn't covered by a current program, you should consider waiting a month or two. New programs start all the time.

As you look over this *CarDeals* report, remember that you may obtain the current issue directly from us. It will be part of the information package that contains the up-to-date dealer invoice prices for the vehicles you're considering, as well as the current version of the Big Picture chart. See Chapter 25 for ordering instructions.

Now let's turn to the third factor that determines the real dealer cost.

DEALER HOLDBACK (THE MONEY NO ONE TALKS ABOUT)

The final piece of this cost puzzle is called dealer holdback, and no one talks about it. If the invoice cost is the last thing the salesman wants you to know, holdback is the last thing the dealer wants you to know, right behind factory-to-dealer incentives. Chances are, he doesn't even discuss it with his salesmen because it's the last thing he wants them thinking about.

For the domestic makes, as well as for a growing number of imports, holdback is one of the significant ways manufacturers put money back into dealers' pockets.

What Is This Thing No One Discusses Openly?

Holdback is a specific percentage of a vehicle's price that is built into the original factory invoice price the dealer pays, held back by the manufacturer for a while, then credited back to the dealer's account after the vehicles are sold, typically quarterly. General Motors, Ford and Chrysler each hold back an amount equal to 3 percent of the retail sticker price (MSRP). While this percentage may seem relatively small, the dollars involved can be significant because even a mid-priced new vehicle costs so much today.

For example, in the 1992 model year a Chevrolet dealer could have sold you a base model two-door 1992 Lumina Coupe at his invoice price and still made $396 from holdback. A Ford dealer could have parted with a four-door Taurus LX Sedan at dealer invoice and still realized over $530 in holdback on the deal. And a Plymouth dealer could have unloaded a two-wheel-drive standard LE Voyager at invoice and received a holdback credit from Chrysler of more than $600.

In effect, holdback is a discount to the dealer which reduces the cost of the vehicle below an inflated dealer invoice price. Think of it as boomerang bucks, money he sends the factory when he pays the original invoice, but which eventually comes back to him.

Because he pays it out up front, he treats it as if it were a cost item, instead of the profit item it really represents when he gets it back from the factory. Since it's a hidden item, it's excluded from the sales transaction. That means he doesn't have to pay a sales commission on it, and it's not on the table for a buyer to negotiate away.

Holdback was instituted in the early 1960s, we understand, as a way to ensure that dealers would have money on hand to pay Uncle Sam at tax time. While that may be one of several benefits to a dealer, holdback clearly benefits manufacturers as well. They've got the use of that money, interest-free, until the next quarterly payment. (In return, they give the dealer an extra couple of weeks to pay for cars received.) And if a dealer owes them money he won't or can't pay, they've always got a chunk of his cash on hand to cover some of that debt.

It's Not Just a Detroit Accounting Item

The practice of holdback has spread to some import brands. Among the Japanese, leaders Toyota/Lexus and Honda/Acura have not adopted the concept, but Mazda, Mitsubishi and Nissan have. Mazda holds back 2 percent of the suggested retail/sticker price; Mitsubishi and Nissan handle it slightly differently, holding back 2 percent of the dealer invoice price. (Infiniti has no holdback.)

Europeans BMW, Jaguar and Volkswagen hold back 2 percent of the sticker price; Rolls-Royce, 3 percent of sticker. Volvo's holdback is $600 on the 240 series, $700 on the 850 series and $900 on the 940 and 960 series. Audi, Mercedes-Benz, Saab and Porsche do not use holdback.

We'll discuss in Chapter 21 exactly how you should use your knowledge of holdback during the negotiating process. Now, though, return to the sample worksheet for our 1993 Speedster on page 73. We've assumed that the fictitious All-American Motor Corporation has the same holdback policy as the three actual domestic manufacturers, and we've entered $532 on the holdback line (3 percent of the $17,720 suggested retail price, excluding the destination charge).

The dealer invoice price. Factory incentives. Holdback. Those are the three key elements that determine the real cost of the vehicle.

There's one other major factor that comes into play each year, after the new models have been introduced. It's called a year-end carryover allowance, another kind of factory-to-dealer payment that we'll discuss in the next chapter.

Many that are first shall be last; and the last shall be first.

—Matthew 19:30

16

Timing

Is Money

Success in any serious endeavor can have a lot to do with being in the right place at the right time. For the new car buyer, timing is money. There are so many timing-related issues in the auto shopping process that we've prepared a separate chapter to focus your attention on all of them.

In this race, getting there last often beats getting there first. Here are some specific illustrations of how the tortoise beats the hare:

1. DON'T MILK THAT DEALER-INCENTIVE COW TILL JUST BEFORE MIDNIGHT

If one of your finalists is covered by a current factory-to-dealer cash incentive program, you'll turn to the *CarDeals* report and check the program's end date. Then you'll time all your serious price negotiation visits so that you'll be able to sign the sales agreement *on one of the last two or three eligible days.*

Here's why: Every promotion program has a beginning, middle and end. As the end approaches, there's a lot of pressure to pump out every sale possible. That's because these programs are often structured so that dealers get higher incentive payments as the number of cars sold increases.

You want to buy from a dealer who's at the highest cash incentive plateau. Your purchase might even be the one that pushes a dealer's entire sales organization up to that plateau. In some programs, a dealer that reaches a certain sales target gets extra cash for all cars sold in the promotion period. This could mean hundreds of dollars for each car previously sold! That store might give quite dramatic discounts as it gets close to its target. That store might be ripe for a knowledgeable shopper to negotiate the buy of a lifetime!

As we noted in the previous chapter, if one or more of your finalist vehicles isn't covered by a consumer or dealer incentive program today, consider waiting a month or two, if you can. New programs start all the time, and you might save an extra thousand dollars or more if you can make one of them work for you.

2. THE END OF THE LINE CAN BE A GREAT PLACE TO STAND

Many people like to buy at the end of the model year, during those year-end cleanout sales. The new models are about to arrive, and they've got to make space for them.

One reason prices are friendlier then is that some manufacturers provide extra money to their dealers to help them sell those year-end leftovers. (They won't get heavy orders for new models if dealers are loaded with last year's cars.) This extra money is called a carryover allowance, and it's a practice employed most often by Detroit.

General Motors and Ford regularly provide a carryover allowance of 5 percent of the sticker price (that's 5 percent of MSRP, not 5 percent of dealer invoice), which they credit to dealers for every previous year's vehicle left in inventory after October 1, the official starting date for each successive model year. On a car or truck with an $18,000 sticker price, that 5 percent represents an additional $900 for you to bargain for.

In practice, this allowance is in effect as soon as the new models arrive, no matter when they're introduced. (For example, in July 1992, Ford introduced its all-new Probe as a 1993 model, providing a 5 percent carryover allowance for the substantial number of slow-selling 1992 Probes still in inventory.) The allowance generally covers all vehicles, but sometimes it excludes hot-selling models in relatively short supply, especially if the new year's versions have only minor changes.

Chrysler has traditionally shunned carryover allowances. In 1991, for the first time since 1978, it offered its dealers the choice of a 5 percent carryover allowance or participation in the July–September consumer and dealer incentive programs. As you might expect, the carryover allowances had few takers among dealers whose basic credo is, "Sell it now and worry about tomorrow later."

One Key Closeout Issue: Slim Pickings   Sometimes year-end pickings can be quite slim, even in a down market. If sales have been depressed for months, both manufacturers and their dealers may write off a model year when it's only half over. Dealers get very selective with their orders as the current year's production winds down, and the factories structure their buildout plans to allow dealers to maintain lean inventories of only the fastest-moving models. They're both hoping to end the old-model year without a glut of leftovers, so they can focus all their resources on the new-model launch in the fall.

This occasional attack of sanity among carmakers is not necessarily good news for shoppers looking for end-of-year bargains. But more often than not, if your heart's set on a model-year leftover, you'll have many to choose from—assuming there are two or three finalists you'd be happy to drive home. Look through the August 7, 1992 *CarDeals* report, printed on pages 172–182 of the Appendix. The 1991 model year had ended ten months earlier, yet you'll note many incentive offers for 1991 Ford and Mercury models, along with the accompanying carryover allowance notation: "and 5% of list price (D)." Those offers wouldn't be there if all the 1991 stock had been sold.

The Other Side of the Year-End Coin   Don't be blinded by those apparently great year-end clearance deals. Savvy buyers understand that they are a mixed blessing. There's a reason Detroit pays its dealers a carryover allowance for last year's cars in inventory after the new models arrive: They're worth considerably less then. Indeed, it's proper to question whether 5 percent of the sticker price is a large enough allowance to cover a vehicle's precipitous drop in value after the new models are introduced.

The day the new models arrived, that old model became last year's car. A year later, when next year's models come out, it'll be a two-year-old. If you sell it then, it will have taken a two-year depreciation hit in one year, no matter how much TLC you've lavished on it.

You should be especially cautious buying last year's closeout if there have been extensive styling changes in the new model. That old, out-of-style car will depreciate even faster than normal when there's a much prettier successor on the highway.

The only way anyone should buy last year's model after the new models arrive is at a big discount from dealer invoice. You should get the entire carryover allowance (5 percent of MSRP) plus all the customer and dealer incentive dollars. Even then, you should plan to keep that car for several years to ride out the negative effect of the car's lower real value when it was purchased.

The moral of the story is that year-end is a great time to buy a bargain, as long as you don't have to sell it in a year or two. And when you trade it, you should do it for another year-end closeout model so you don't get stuck selling low and buying high.

Returning to the worksheet for our imaginary 1993 All-American Speedster on page 73, you'll note that we've entered an assumed year-end carryover allowance of $886 on the appropriate line. (That's 5 percent of the $17,720 sticker price, excluding delivery charges.) If you were shopping for that car after the 1994 model was introduced, that 5 percent would be an important element in your negotiation.

3. GETTING THERE FIRST
CAN BE AN EXPENSIVE TRIP

Remember the Mazda MX-5 Miata. (That's a warning, not a question.) The Miata came out in 1990 to rave reviews, with a sticker price of $13,800 and just enough cars to reach from your kitchen to your dining room, end to end. Mazda dealers loved it! Many put their ADM (additional dealer mark-up) stickers on every one and doubled or tripled their gross profit per car.

And the newspapers were still full of consumers' buy-and-sell offers at prices from $20,000. Talk about being in new-car heat!

Today you can buy a Miata for a price no higher than MSRP, and have just as much fun driving it as the folks who paid an extra $5,000 or $10,000 in 1990. You just can't be the first on your block to own one.

Supply and Demand: It's the Law Whatever the item, if more people want it than can get it, those who get it will pay for the privilege. World Series tickets, Super Bowl hotel rooms, the first 2,000 Mazda Miatas . . . you name it.

This truth works against the car buyer at the beginning of the model year, though usually less dramatically than in the case of a hot new car like the Miata. From October through December, when a new model is in relatively short supply, the dealer may not accept the same price he will later in the year, when the only things standing in line are the cars on his lot.

Bugs Aren't Just on Windshields There's another reason to avoid a brand-new model in the early months of production: bugs. Even in this era of dramatically improved product quality, it frequently takes auto manu-facturers several months or more to get the hang of making glitch-free products.

Look at the vexing little problems that plagued GM's Saturn in its first year: A recall for defective seats. A recall for a corrosive engine coolant. Early buyers' complaints about noisy, vibrating engines.

Saturn was launched with great ballyhoo in the fall of 1990, following a $5 billion capital investment and seven years of meticulous planning. Yet many say that what Saturn did best in 1991 was correct problems with great consumer and public relations sensitivity.

By 1992, the bugs had been eliminated and the Saturn buyer could anticipate a glitch-free vehicle. But Saturn's early pratfalls illustrate that even a company determined to get it right can stumble coming out of the blocks. And the wise buyer will always count to ten before purchasing a brand-new vehicle.

4. TALK TURKEY LATE IN THE MONTH, AND LATE IN THE DAY

As it says in the song, "There is a time to every purpose under heaven."

- The time to kick tires and take test drives and do research is during the first three weeks of the month.
- The time for serious negotiation is during the last week of the month.

Every sales organization lives or dies from month to month. Auto manufacturers report sales monthly, and they focus their dealers on the same time frame, using quotas or incentives or just plain fear to motivate them. The dealers pass along the quotas, the incentives and the fear to their sales managers.

That usually makes the end of the month the best time to buy. Your purchase could be the one that puts them over the top, and you might strike a terrific bargain.

Some of the smartest shoppers always buy their new cars during the last hour of the last day of December. That way salesmen can't waste their time with their system games. (More on these in the next chapter.) They carry a cashier's check for the maximum amount they're prepared to pay. And they claim they always leave with both the car they want and the dealer's check for the difference between their maximum and the lower price they really paid.

Here's another tactic that works. If it's the last weekend of the month, and your price negotiation is stalled on a number that's too high, tell the salesman that you're going home to sleep on it, that you'll be back next weekend. Many times you'll find that the price will drop magically, just as you head for the door.

The exception to this end-of-month rule would be if the last days of a relevant factory-to-dealer incentive program came at a different time. Given all the incentive activity in the market today, there's probably more buyer leverage in timing those specific factory programs just right. (You'll note, however, that most programs seem to finish at the end of a month, or a few days later.)

5. AN EMPTY SHOWROOM
CAN BE FULL OF OPPORTUNITY

If you're the only one there, your chances of striking a terrific deal may be enhanced dramatically. So don't be afraid to shop "the middles"—the middle of the week, the middle of a blizzard or deluge, even the middle of the Christmas season (as long as you don't tell them it's a Christmas present). And car stores can be particularly accommodating in January and

February, when most people are paying off holiday bills and not thinking of buying new cars and trucks.

6. "THE STRONGEST OF WARRIORS ARE THESE TWO: TIME AND PATIENCE." (Leo Tolstoi, *War and Peace*)

If you forget everything else in this chapter, remember this: Time is always on your side, not theirs. In a waiting game, the loser will be the one who needs the deal the most.

The sooner you need to have a new car, the more it's going to cost. If that's today, or this weekend, you'd better have a Brink's truck for a trade-in. A loaded Brink's truck.

But if you can wait 'em out, the time will come when they'll want a sale even more than you want a new car. That offer they refused weeks ago has a way of looking much better in the cold, hard glare of the end of another month. Sometimes just one more sale—even a below-invoice sale—can be very important to a dealer.

All it takes is time, a luxury that dealers seldom have. If you've got it, use it.

17

The Games Salesmen Play

We must take a hard look at the way we market our cars ... and the way we approach customers on the floor and present the deal. Until we address these issues, the image of new-car dealers will remain about the same—awful.

—President of the National Automobile Dealers Association at its convention in Dallas, February 1992

Before you finalize your approach to negotiating price, you should be aware of some of the things car salesmen do to control the sales situation and to get you to do what they want, which is to buy today, at a price that maximizes their profit. Watch for these old favorites:

THE BUDDY SYSTEM

This salesman is on your side; it's you and him against "them." He'll do his best to get management to give you a great deal. He leaves the room a lot, only to return to say they wouldn't buy a price that low, they need more. (You're at the blood bank, negotiating with Dracula through a zombie, and the only blood there is yours.)

This is a game, and a transparent one at that. Don't let him play it. Tell him you appreciate his concern for you, but you want to talk to "them," not their messenger. If the game doesn't stop, walk out.

THE SILENT TREATMENT

This is the Buddy System's first cousin. The salesman leaves you in the room (they call it "the box") for long periods of time while he's "negotiating for you" with his sales manager.

In reality, that salesman probably knows exactly how low they'll go to sell you that car. While he's away you can bet he's drinking coffee with the guys, talking about last night's date or next week's fishing trip. He'll eventually come back with a "bump" (an increase) over your last offer, because "they" didn't buy it.

The game here is to keep you there (so you can't be at any other car store) and to wear you down. They want you so frustrated by the delays that you'll sign anything just to get it finished.

The first time he gets up to leave, tell him nicely but firmly that you've been through this before, that you appreciate the position he's in, but you're not going to sit there for a lot of back-and-forth negotiations with a phantom. Say that if he's not back in five minutes with someone you can negotiate with directly, you've got three other dealers you plan to visit and he can expect to find you gone. Then look him straight in the eye and hit the beeper on your digital wristwatch.

THE BUMP-AND-GRIND

This is a more systematic version of the Silent Treatment. The waiting periods aren't as long, but you're being played up and down like a yo-yo by someone you don't even get to see.

Your buddy, the salesman, leaves the box after introducing you to his sales manager, who'll be "the closer." (You've been T.O.'d, or taken over, by a more senior salesman.) This guy is usually still a middleman, taking your concessions out to some phantom who scribbles notes you can't read and returning to ask if you can "just help him out" to the tune of another $50 a month so he can close the deal. (Over four years, that $50 a month will cost you $2,400, and the closer will get 10 to 25 percent of that "bump.")

Your response to the Bump-and-Grind should be the same as the Silent Treatment. Either it stops now or you walk to another car store, now.

THE LOWBALL OPENER

Some stores will have the salesman quote you an initial price that sounds too good to be true—sometimes over the phone, as a way to get you into the showroom. *You can be sure that it is.* When you agree to that number, he'll return with a "bump," saying they wouldn't go for it. This is just another way to draw you into the game.

If you think he's lowballing, tell him that you've been through this before, that you expect him to return again and say management wouldn't buy it, and that if that's the game they want to play, you've got three other stores to visit and you'll leave as soon as he returns with the predicted news flash.

Tell him that you want to talk to someone who can negotiate with you directly, now, or you're leaving.

Note: Another variation is the Lowball Send-off. The salesman knows you're going to go out and shop around, so he gives you an unrealistically low quote that no dealer would match, including his. When you leave, he's got you "out on a ball," and he knows you'll be back. When you eventually return to take him up on that lowball offer, you learn that it was too good to be true. By then, he hopes, you'll be so tired of running around trying to beat it that you'll be ready to make any deal he wants.

THE CASTING DIRECTOR

This salesman wants to typecast you as soon as he can. Anything you say will be used against you.

• Are you "a payment buyer," someone who cares only that the monthly payment is something you can handle? He can fix you right up, with a deal that maximizes both his profit and the length of your loan. (But the monthly payments will be close to what you said you could handle.)

Don't ever talk to a car salesman about monthly payments. If you've done your homework, you already know what kind of financing and payments you're planning, and it's none of his business.

• Are you "an allowance buyer," someone who's focused only on the trade-in allowance they'll offer on your used car? He can fix you right up, with a deal that maximizes both your trade-in allowance and his profit.

Don't ever talk to a car salesman about a trade-in allowance. Go back and review Chapters 4 through 9. By now, you're too smart to fall for this one. As you've already learned, the less you tell the salesman, the better off you'll be.

THE CHECK-IN CLERK

In many dealerships, the first thing a salesman will want to do is fill out a data card, with your name, address and phone numbers. He'll add the sticker price information on the car you want, including all the options. Then he'll want to add information about your trade-in, like the vehicle identification number and the mileage.

Then, as long as he's writing, he'll ask your date of birth, driver's license number and social security number. (They'll need this to run a credit report on you if you end up financing through the dealer. But they want to run the report now, both to be sure you're not a deadbeat and to see which other dealers have checked your credit recently, so they'll know where you've been shopping.)

No deal has been discussed yet, no prices mentioned, but he wants all this personal data. He'll pass the data card to his superior as soon as he leaves the box.

This is a car store, not a hotel or personnel office! And you're not registering for a room or applying for a job. At this stage, you're just starting a dialogue that might or might not lead to a purchase. *Until you've got a deal that* you *can agree to, all you should tell him is your name.* Even if you end up buying there, they won't need most of that information unless you're financing through the dealer.

THE HOSTAGE TAKER

Many salesmen will ask for a deposit check to accompany your offer when they take it to their superior. They call it evidence that you're a serious buyer. But for them, *that check is a hostage that will keep you at their store and prevent you from shopping around for a better deal.*

Smile nicely, but tell him that you're not writing a deposit check for anything until you and they have agreed on a deal for everything. And that if his store requires a deposit check simply to negotiate a deal, you're sure you can find one that doesn't. The rule will change quickly.

Incidentally, the keys to your current car can also become an effective hostage. Salesmen have been known to "misplace" them, and even to refuse to return them when you ask. At this point you're not there to talk about a trade-in; *keep the keys in your pocket or purse.*

THE LIMITED-TIME OFFER

You might negotiate to a price that sounds pretty good, but this is only your first store. You plan to go through the same drill at two or three other dealerships. You tell him that it's a big decision for you, that you want to think about it overnight. You thank him and get up to leave. The salesman then says, in a bit of a huff, that if you leave he can't give you the same price tomorrow. (He's upset; his mission is to close you now.)

Call his bluff! Smile and say that's too bad, because if it's true he's going to miss the opportunity to sell you a car. You are leaving, you've got several other dealers you haven't talked with yet, and you're sure one of them will have a different attitude.

Then ask him again if he really meant that he wouldn't sell you that car at that price tomorrow, so you'll be sure not to bother him.

Remember Reality 101: There's another deal that good, and probably better, around the next corner.

Then remember Salesman's Reality 101: If you don't buy, he doesn't sell. And if he doesn't sell, he doesn't eat.

MR. OBNOXIOUS

Chances are, you'll end up with a given salesman just because it's his turn. His number is up when you walk in, and you become his "up."

Chemistry is important. If you quickly find he's someone you'd rather not deal with, excuse yourself to go to the rest room. Then ask someone where you can find the sales manager, walk in and tell him you've got a problem he's going to have to solve, or you're going to have to leave. That salesman is not someone you can work with, and you'd like to talk to someone else. Then go to the rest room.

When you return, you'll meet a new, less obnoxious salesperson— maybe even the sales manager himself.

If a Cavalier is advertised for $7,999, you had better load it up with extras or your head is on the chopping block.

—Salesperson participating in a sales certification training program developed by the National Automobile Dealers Association (printed in *Automotive News*, April 13, 1992)

18

Back-End Options: Just Say No

The *Random House Webster's College Dictionary* says that "option" means "the power or right of choosing." It also says that "optional" means "not required."

Car salesmen have a different dictionary. Theirs says "option" means "any additional equipment or accessories they can stick on a new vehicle that are of maximum profitability to the car store."

It's bad enough that manufacturers load their vehicles with packages of optional equipment, some of which you may not need or want. At least they typically give you a package price, so that you're not paying that much for the things you don't want.

But then the car stores add their own high-profit dealer options on the back end. You'll find them hung all over the vehicles you're shopping. That doesn't mean you have to buy them.

THE OTHER STICKER

Your first clue that something's up is the other sticker on the window. It's often designed to look just like the Monroney, complete with an illustration of that little gas pump. It's not; *it's the car store's sticker.*

There's often more profit potential for the car store on that sticker than on the basic car itself, but most of the items there won't add a dime's worth of value or utility. Let's replay a few of the Greatest Hits.

"THE MOP 'N GLOW"

This group includes things like "rust-preventive undercoating," "fabric guard protection spray," "paint sealant," "sound shield," decorative striping, mud flaps and deluxe floor mats. This strange entourage frequently masquerades under important-sounding names like Optional Environmental Protection Package.

This little protection package can carry a retail price from $300–$400 to as much as $1,000 or more. Its cost to the car store is peanuts—typically under $100. You need this stuff like Madonna needs a face-lift!

• Let's start with *"rust-preventive undercoating."* Today's new vehicles carry very substantial anti-corrosion warranties from just about all manufacturers. The domestics typically cover 6 or 7 years, or 100,000 miles, whichever comes first. The major imports cover 5 to 7 years, usually with unlimited mileage. (Check the coverage for your finalists.)

Probably the best argument against buying dealer rustproofing is that many factories recommend against it! Here's a quote from a General Motors warranty:

> Some after-manufacture rustproofing may create a potential environment which reduces the corrosion resistance designed and built into your vehicle. Depending upon application technique, [it] could result in damage or failure of some electrical or mechanical systems of your vehicle. Repairs to correct damage or malfunctions caused by

after-manufacture rustproofing are not covered under any of your GM new vehicle warranties.

Any questions?

• *"Fabric guard protection spray."* You call this Scotchgard. A fourteen-ounce can of 3M's Scotchgard® sells for about $6 in your supermarket and covers 14 to 21 square feet of fabric. Three cans should do the trick.

• *"Paint sealant."* Today's automotive paint jobs are technological wonders compared to twenty years ago, when additional protection may have been beneficial. The primary thing it benefits now is the size of the salesmen's bonus pool.

The bottom line: Tell the salesman to leave the Mop 'n Glo in Aisle 9, where it belongs. Tell him either he throws in the $79.95 cost of the total package for free or finds you a car without it, or you'll find another dealer who will. (In fact, you'd rather buy a car without it.)

DEALER PREPARATION

You may see a charge for dealer preparation. You shouldn't pay it. Virtually all manufacturers include predelivery preparation in the car's base price.

ADM, ADP, AND AMV

Printed boldly on the Other Sticker, these abbreviations represent the most arrogant form of customer-fleecing. They stand for additional dealer markup, additional dealer profit and additional market value. They used to be added to any car in relatively high demand and short supply, particularly imports.

In the tough sales climate of the 1990s, most car stores have dropped these extra charges, but they're not extinct. You'll find them on virtually all new vehicles at some stores. The added markups can range from $1,000 on a $9,000 pickup truck to $6,000 on a $30,000 sports car. What they provide, of course, is an artificially higher asking price from which to start negotiating.

If you see them, tell the salesman you're going to ignore them. If he won't cooperate, either you've got a dealer who's not living in the real world or you're looking at the rare vehicle whose demand exceeds today's supply (like that Dodge Viper which the dealer thought would sell for $20,000 over the sticker price).

Our advice would be to shop several dealers to find one without "A-words" on his stickers, or to wait a few months for supply to catch up with demand. (It always does.) And remember that a car sold with an "A-word" sticker won't be worth a nickel more at trade-in time than the same car without that initial surcharge.

SOME OPTIONS ARE HARD TO AVOID

Some options, both manufacturer- and dealer-installed, just seem to come with the territory. That's often true on newer models that are in relatively short supply. For example, for a while it was difficult to find a Honda Accord station wagon without a relatively expensive dealer-installed roof rack. If you were a prospect for that car, you learned to grin and bear it. What's a station wagon without a roof rack, anyway?

Here's one option you should avoid: the car store's logo, either drilled into or glued onto the back end of your new car. Make sure you tell the salesman you won't accept delivery of any vehicle with his store's advertising attached to it. (The exception to this rule is a license frame plate bearing the dealer's name, which you can remove easily. As you'll learn in Chapter 20, this can be a useful long-term ally.)

INDIVIDUAL FACTORY ORDERS: THE SOLUTION TO THE OPTION GAME?

As you may know, domestic cars can be special-ordered from the manufacturers. Many advisors recommend this as the way to get a vehicle equipped exactly to your order. And perhaps there is something special about having one built just for you.

Any dealer would be happy to take your order. It's an easy sale and, unlike his regular inventory, he doesn't have to invest anything in your car. He may even accept a low-profit deal, just because it'll help his "turn and earn" record. (Many dealers are allotted cars based on past sales performance. Moving a lot of cars, especially in a poor sales year, will help ensure that he'll get all he needs in better years, when popular cars are scarcer and markups are higher.)

Nevertheless, we don't think special ordering is the best way to buy a car today, for these reasons:

✓ For openers, it'll take 6 to 8 weeks or more to get delivery, if you're lucky. A lot of things can happen to your current car in that time, none of them good.

✓ You may not be able to predict a realistic delivery date, especially if you order in the second half of the model year. When sales are slower, manufacturers periodically shut down selected factories for a week or more to avoid excess inventory buildup. The plants selected may include the one that makes your car.

✓ It's not as easy as it used to be to get the exact options you want, even with a factory order. Manufacturers don't really customize orders. Many of them sell certain popular options only in packages, which may contain things you don't want.

✓ You probably won't be able to take advantage of either consumer or dealer incentive offers with a factory-ordered car. The consumer programs typically require that you take delivery from dealer stock, and the dealer programs are usually for cars sold and delivered within certain dates.

So you'll pay the $500 to $1,000+ built into the price of the car to cover these programs, but you'll receive no benefit.

✓ If you're adamant about getting a specifically equipped car, and if the car is built that way, a dealer may be able to find that exact car for you at another dealership. All dealers have access to a computerized inventory of vehicles in their sales zone, which generally covers several states. They frequently work a dealer exchange to get a specific car. (Note, however, that on a dealer trade, the dealer who sends the car retains the factory holdback dollars on the vehicle. That may mean that your dealer—the receiving dealer—will be less flexible on price than he would be for a vehicle from his own inventory.)

✓ Finally, we think you've got a better shot at negotiating an attractive price on a car that's in a dealer's stock than on a special-ordered car. He's paying interest to keep that car in inventory, so he's highly motivated to get it off his lot and into your garage. (In 1991, the average car store spent over $225 in interest per new car sold.)

Here's how to estimate how long a car has been in a dealer's inventory. Look for the federally mandated manufacturer's sticker or plate that shows the month and year of manufacture. It will also carry these words: "This vehicle conforms to all applicable federal motor vehicle safety, bumper and theft prevention standards in effect on the date of manufacture shown above." It's usually placed inside the jamb of the driver's door, but may also be under the hood—on the firewall between the engine and passenger compartments—or on one of the wheel wells.

If the date of manufacture was more than four months ago, you may assume the dealer is particularly anxious to sell that vehicle and might accept a lower offer than for a car that just arrived on his lot.

Ethically, we should quote payments on a stripped vehicle to customers. But that cuts out the Finance and Insurance manager, so we are told at meetings to quote loaded payments. You can always come down, but you can't go up.

—Salesperson participating in a sales certification training program developed by the National Automobile Dealers Association (printed in *Automotive News*, April 13, 1992)

Are Extended Warranties Warranted?

The sale of an extended warranty contract, which pays for repairs that occur after the factory warranty runs out, is a big back-end profit item for every car store. These contracts typically cost $500 to $1,000 and can exceed $2,000, depending on what they cover and what the traffic (you) will bear.

You can expect to get a strong recommendation to buy one, frequently from the store's F&I manager. Watch out for this guy. You've escaped from "the closing box," but you're in the clutches of another commissioned salesman. He's a low-pressure operator who wants you to trust his advice as you would your father's. He's not your father; he's interested in your wallet, not your welfare.

BE PREPARED FOR THIS ONE

You should determine beforehand whether this purchase makes sense for you. The decision hinges on your answers to these two questions:

1. What's the basic bumper-to-bumper warranty on the car you're buying?

2. How long do you plan to keep the car, and about how many miles will you drive it?

MOST BASIC WARRANTIES ARE NOW CLOSE TO PARITY

The old standard, a bumper-to-bumper warranty of one year or 12,000 miles (whichever comes first), has become a thing of the past, thanks to Toyota, Honda and Nissan. The Japanese Big Three provide a basic warranty of 3 years or 36,000 miles, and starting with the 1992 models, Detroit's Big Three finally matched their key competitors.

Both Ford and Chrysler maintained that ancient 12-month/12,000-mile warranty on most vehicles through the 1991 model year! By contrast, virtually all 1991 General Motors products had a 36-month/50,000-mile warranty.

• The combination of dealer pressure and a tough competitive climate helped Ford see the light. In May 1991, representatives of the Ford Division's 4,500 dealers lobbied hard for warranty parity with GM and the big imports. As one dealer put it, "We can't compete with the Hondas and Toyotas of the world. If Ford is sincere about quality, it should have warranties to back it up."

In response, Ford upped the basic warranty for Ford and Mercury vehicles to 36 months/36,000 miles, starting with the 1992 models. This improved coverage may affect the purchase of extended warranties. Historically, 45 percent of Ford customers who finance through a dealership have bought extended service contracts. With the new bumper-to-bumper protection, we'd expect that percentage to drop.

• Chrysler responded to these competitive moves by offering its customers a choice, starting with the 1992 models—either a new bumper-to-bumper warranty of 36 months/36,000 miles or the old 12-month/12,000-mile basic warranty combined with the company's traditional 7-year/70,000-mile powertrain warranty. (Powertrain warranties cover the things that make the car go—the engine, transmission and drivetrain.)

Among the domestics, Chrysler is now the only company offering free powertrain coverage extending beyond the basic warranty. But that doesn't necessarily mean that Chrysler's powertrain combination is the best warranty choice for those buying its products.

In the past, powertrain warranties covered most of the major problems you might encounter after the original warranty expired because the only really expensive repair bills came from powertrain problems.

Today's automobiles, however, are loaded with complicated new systems that have nothing to do with the things that make the car go. Electronic instrument panels with all kinds of gadgets. Power equipment options. Anti-lock braking systems. Cruise control. Sophisticated steering and suspension systems.

Diagnosing and fixing problems with these systems is more difficult and expensive than it was with their predecessors. And when they need fixing after the basic warranty period, it's your money that's on the line.

If it were our decision, we'd choose Chrysler's 36-month/36,000-mile bumper-to-bumper warranty option over the 12-month/12,000-mile + powertrain alternative. (You can bet that Chrysler would rather see us choose the other option. The longer bumper-to-bumper program probably costs them close to 50 percent more in warranty claims. Wouldn't you rather have them pay that 50 percent?)

• Starting with the 1992 model year, *General Motors* lowered its warranty on most models from 36 months/50,000 miles to 36 months/36,000 miles, in line with the Japanese and the revised Ford and Chrysler coverage policies.

Worth noting: Some import makes have a separate powertrain warranty extending beyond the basic bumper-to-bumper coverage. Toyota and Nissan, for example, cover powertrain components for 5 years or 60,000 miles, whichever comes first. This makes their warranties somewhat better, overall, than any domestic company's.

With most major manufacturers now at or near parity on basic warranty coverage, the decision as to whether to buy an extended warranty contract will depend on how long you'll keep the vehicle and how far you'll drive it.

THIS CAN BE EXPENSIVE OVER-INSURANCE

Remember, these extended warranties don't kick in until the basic coverage kicks out. If you buy a car with an initial factory warranty of 36 months or 36,000 miles, your extension coverage doesn't begin until either mile number 36,001 or the first day of month 37.

Will you keep the car that long and/or drive it that far? If you will, how much longer and farther do you think you'll own and drive it? If you're not sure, it may be better to put $500 aside as self-insurance against a Big Bucks repair bill. (This alternative may be very attractive if you're buying a Toyota or Nissan product that comes with an extended powertrain warranty.)

But if you're planning to drive the car until the wheels fall off, an extended warranty can be a wise investment. Note that you probably don't have to make this decision when you buy the car. In most cases, you may purchase this contract anytime within the first 12 months or 12,000 miles. You're likely to buy it more cheaply, however, as part of the initial vehicle purchase, when you'll have more negotiating leverage. When you return to buy it later, they'll know it's something you really want and try to get top dollar for it.

FOUR IMPORTANT SUGGESTIONS
FOR CONTRACT BUYERS

1. *Buy only a factory-backed warranty,* not one that's backed only by a third party. In recent years, several third-party underwriters have gone bankrupt. Many unwary consumers were left holding worthless contracts that neither the factories nor the dealers would honor.

2. *Read the fine print.* Understand which parts are not covered, whether there's a deductible charge per repair, whether the contract is transferable if you sell the car, and whether you'll get any money back if you cancel.

3. *The price is as negotiable as the price of the car.* Salesmen will tell you that an expensive post-warranty repair could cost you over $2,000, making this $1,000+ "insurance policy" a good investment. What they won't tell you is that this $1,000+ extended coverage contract costs them only $200 to $500.

This is one of the highest-margin items any car store sells. If you want it, offer *half* the asking price, and don't pay more than *two thirds.* Many dealers today would rather sell it and make $200 than not sell it and make nothing.

4. *"Use it or lose it."* With both the initial bumper-to-bumper factory coverage and the extended protection, why have it if you don't use it? This question is especially relevant as you approach the end of the coverage periods.

During the last month or the last 1,000 miles of coverage, ask your dealer's service department to go over the car thoroughly to determine whether any major problems are on the horizon. Request that they do something now about these problems, while your car is still under warranty. A good service operation will be glad to do this for a regular customer.

20

Two roads diverged in a wood, and I—
I took the one less traveled by,
And that has made all the difference.

—Robert Frost,
"The Road Not Taken"

Choosing Your Dealer Finalists

Now it's time to pick the dealers you'll visit for serious price negotiations on your finalist vehicles. Given what we've told you so far, this may seem as if we're throwing you a curve ball. We're not; this is simply one more aspect of smart buying.

The dealer you want to buy from will not necessarily be the one who'll give you the best price, but the one who'll give you the best service.

Your dealer finalists should be those that satisfy two key requirements:

1. They're geographically desirable, reasonably close to either your home or workplace.

2. They've got service departments with above-average track records.

The convenience factor is obvious. The last thing you need is a 40-mile round trip for basic warranty work. The "service-over-price" factor is less obvious. Indeed, it contradicts the counsel of such esteemed advisors as *Consumer Reports.*

CAN *CONSUMER REPORTS* BE WRONG ABOUT ANYTHING? (IS THE SKY FALLING?)

Let's look at the advice they've given. In the April 1991 Annual Auto Issue, *Consumer Reports* cites the experiences of people who traveled 70 and 80 miles from home, respectively, to buy new vehicles. These cases were positioned as successful shopping experiences, and from the standpoint of getting a somewhat lower price they apparently were. But we question whether these people made good long-term choices.

Consumer Reports' attitude is apparently colored by its view of the warranty repair issue. Here's what Consumer Reports Books says on that subject on page 6 of its *1991–92 New Car Buying Guide:*

> WARRANTY REPAIRS. Dealers for most car makes are required to perform repairs covered by warranty for all cars of that nameplate, no matter where the cars were purchased. So having repairs on a car bought [somewhere else] rarely should be a problem. Dealers make money on repairs regardless of who sold the car in the first place.

These statements are both true. The question is whether they mean, as *Consumer Reports* concludes, that you'll "rarely" have a problem having warranty work done on a car bought somewhere else.

We have great respect for *Consumer Reports'* work when they're evaluating things, like toasters and vacuum cleaners and even automobiles. But automobile service has more to do with people than with things.

A TOASTER IS A TOASTER, BUT A CAR IS YOUR LIFE

You need a good ongoing relationship with a dealer's service department if you're going to get your money's worth from the second most expensive purchase of your life, the machine you count on daily to take you where you need to go. With the right dealer and the right service department, you can get so much more than your money's worth that the $500 or so you might save buying the car somewhere else will look like very small change—especially when you need warranty work.

Your best shot at establishing the right relationship with a dealer's service department will come from buying your car there and having all its service performed there. The reason lies in this basic economic fact: Today the average car store makes most of its profit by selling parts and service, not by selling cars.

According to the National Automobile Dealers Association (NADA), in 1991 the average dealer's parts and service sales were about $2 million. This represented roughly 15 percent of a dealership's total sales, but accounted for over 80 percent of total profits! If parts and service is the golden goose, you can bet that dealers are going to protect that goose any way they can to maximize its profits.

And what *Consumer Reports* doesn't tell you is that *dealers make less profit on factory-paid warranty repairs than on regular, customer-paid work.* Here's how dealers typically are compensated for warranty work:

• First, while the factories might pay dealers the same hourly wage rate for warranty work that you pay for nonwarranty work, they typically set specific time limits for almost every type of repair and won't compensate dealers for additional time spent. For many legitimate reasons, including difficulty in pinpointing problems quickly, the time spent can exceed the time allowed, and dealers frequently end up "eating" a lot of that un-reimbursed time.

• Second, and probably more important, the manufacturers allow dealers only a minimal markup on warranty parts, thus limiting a major profit opportunity. You may assume that the retail markup on parts that you pay for ranges from 50 to 100 percent, depending on the part and the dealer, with the average markup about 60 percent. But the domestic and import automakers, which profit substantially by selling the dealer those same parts, have traditionally paid him a much smaller wholesale markup on those used in warranty work—typically 30 percent.

This issue became a major source of dealer dissatisfaction in 1992. As one Texas Ford dealer put it, "There's a disincentive—get that word: DIS-IN-CEN-TIVE—to do warranty work. Ford Motor Company does nothing but pay lip service to customer satisfaction."

A study conducted for NADA by consulting firm Booz, Allen and Hamilton, Inc. added fuel to the dealers' fire. It concluded that this limited parts markup policy costs the average dealership about $63,000 annually on warranty work, and that the figure could grow to almost $90,000 annually as warranty coverage is extended.

But it would cost Detroit's Big Three many billions each to pay dealers full retail on all warranty parts. With profits still hard to come by, no automaker is in a position to swallow pills that big in one gulp.

Responding to dealer pressure, however, automakers have taken smaller first steps. Ford agreed to increase the markup to 35 percent on 1993 models and 40 percent on 1994 models. Toyota followed by raising its markup to 45 percent on 1993 models. On January 1, 1993, Chrysler started paying a 40 percent markup for warranty parts for its five newest vehicles—the Jeep Grand Cherokee, Dodge Viper, Dodge Intrepid, Eagle Vision and Chrysler Concorde—while sticking to 30 percent for all other vehicles. GM will go to 40 percent, starting with its 1994 models. Other manufacturers have announced similar improvements.

Even if most companies follow suit, the new markups will still be below the levels dealers want. The issue of dealer profitability on warranty work is likely to remain a bone of contention throughout the 1990s.

But wait, there's more!

• The paperwork blizzard required of dealers to document and claim reimbursement for warranty repairs is a costly nightmare. (If you've ever signed off on warranty work, you know.) And, of course, the speed of factory reimbursement doesn't compare with the instant payment received from customers for nonwarranty work.

• Finally, to add insult to injury, many manufacturers require that dealers save the replaced parts so that they can check them later, if they wish, to ensure that those parts did, indeed, warrant replacing.

You don't need to be a rocket scientist to understand why no service manager in his right mind would want to load his shop on any given day with warranty work, especially for customers who bought their cars somewhere else.

ARE THERE TWO CLASSES OF OWNERSHIP?

Whenever one dealer has a better service operation than others selling the same make, the word gets around. People start using that better service facility more, especially when their factory warranties have expired and they're spending their own money. (That's why there are a dozen cars in line at 7 a.m. at some dealerships and only two or three customers at the same-make dealership three miles down the road.)

So what does the manager of that busy first-class service operation do when you call to schedule warranty work on a car you bought somewhere else?

• First, he checks his schedule. If it's crowded, he may put you off to a slow day later in the week, when he'd rather have warranty work than no work. (But he'd probably find a way to squeeze in a regular customer.)

• Perhaps, if he takes you, he might tell you he's not sure he can get it out today. (You could end up at the end of the line if enough regular customers come in.) And you may get one of those phone calls saying, "We can't finish the job today because we need to send out for a part."

But more important, long-term, is what he doesn't do, which is go out of his way to do anything special for you. He'll follow the letter of the law, but he probably won't bend it in your favor, as he might for regulars.

To illustrate, let's look at some things a good service operation can do to keep its regular customers happy.

CREATIVE RULE-BENDING

Has this ever happened to you? You take your car in for regular service and learn when you pick it up that they've fixed something important, something that you didn't even know was broken. Since this expensive work is covered by your warranty, you're pleased that the service department was so thorough.

You'll probably be surprised to learn that there's a reasonable chance that they didn't make that repair to your car, they made it to the car of another good customer whose warranty, perhaps, had recently expired. They simply charged the factory paperwork to your (in-warranty) car. Neither you nor the other customer knew this, but you both drove home happy.

The manufacturers' service people will never admit that they condone this action, but they want happy customers, too. A few bad dealer service operations can affect their company's overall consumer satisfaction ratings, which, in turn, can affect sales. Common sense says they're likely to look the other way when the rules get bent occasionally by a dealer who keeps his (and their) customers happy.

Here's another example of how a good service operation can make life simpler for a valued customer. Have you ever had a car perform badly all day, but when you took it to the dealer it ran beautifully, and their computer analyzer said all the parts were fine?

You had "an intermittent problem," which is often the lead-in to a terminal problem, but because the computer said the part was okay, the dealer couldn't replace it under warranty. (Remember, the factories want them to save the replaced parts so they can check their condition and refuse payment if they still work.)

A first-class service department may handle this more creatively. They don't want customers' problems to reappear after they've declared their vehicles fixed. They've seen this complaint before, and they know which part is causing the problem. They decide to replace it now, despite what the computer says. To eliminate any potential reimbursement problem, they'll hook up that used part to their Godzilla Electric Chair to guarantee that it'll be a dead soldier, if and when the manufacturer tests it.

We're not saying these things are done routinely every day. But they are done, and they're more likely to be done for the most valued customers. And that's why, if you have your car serviced where you bought it, it's a good idea to leave the dealer's license plate frame on the car as a reminder to his service people that you're one of them.

Incidentally, a good service department doesn't necessarily have to bend the rules to accomplish small miracles for you. Many times they'll simply call the manufacturer's regional service manager and ask for special favors for good customers. And the factory people are more likely to grant favors to a service operation that causes them fewer problems.

THE PERVASIVE POWER OF THE CSI

As everyone with a TV set must know by now, CSI stands for Customer Satisfaction Index. In the competitive market they face today, both the manufacturers and their dealers are in the CSI business, not the automobile business. CSI scores are important on several levels:

• On one level, J. D. Power and Associates' CSI data is publicized nationally, providing an important halo for the auto makes that score well. The leaders celebrate their performance in advertising, and consumers are influenced positively. (A good example is Buick's sales resurgence after outscoring every other American car in the 1989 Initial Quality Survey.)

• On another level, recognizing the critical importance of satisfied customers, the manufacturers are conducting regular in-depth research among their own buyers to establish CSI ratings for each individual dealership. This helps them identify rotten apples that might spoil the whole crop.

It also gives them a basis for rewarding top performers. BMW bases dealer bonus payments importantly on customer satisfaction, not just sales. Infiniti has paid its dealers $25,000 or more each for their quarterly customer satisfaction scores. And Chrysler has established a dealer cash incentive system in which the payments are based on a combination of sales performance and consumer satisfaction ratings. (This is what prompted Chairman Lee Iacocca to quip, "It seems a helluva note in life that we must pay a dealer to be nice to his customers.")

Individual dealer CSI scores also provide a rationale for allocating scarce product. For example, in order to qualify to sell Dodge's expensive, limited-volume Viper sports car, dealers were required to have a minimum CSI score on Chrysler's internal rating scale.

• Finally, a dealer's CSI in his current stores is a key factor in determining whether he'll be chosen by another manufacturer when it's expanding its dealer base.

Many dealers today are mega-dealers who own several different franchises. For example, of the 500 Mitsubishi dealers at the start of 1991, 20 percent also had Chevrolet franchises, 15 percent Toyota, 15 percent Nissan, 14 percent Hyundai, 14 percent Oldsmobile, 14 percent Honda and 13 percent Ford. The average Mitsubishi dealer owned 2.7 franchises. And only the ones with above-average CSI scores are likely to get additional makes to sell.

The Great CSI Scores Are Built on Service, Not Sales

Once you drive that car home, your longer-term impressions of satisfaction with the selling dealer will reflect how well a dealer's service operation treats you and your expensive baby. Smart dealers understand that "price may bring 'em in, but service brings 'em back." These dealers work harder than others to keep customers happy, and that extra effort helps keep their overall CSI scores among the leaders. These are the kinds of dealers you want.

Assuming you're sold on this point of view, it's time to narrow your choices.

CHOOSING YOUR FINALISTS

You can learn something useful from the dealership experiences of friends and neighbors driving the same make. But you'll gain the most insight by doing your own research, relatively painlessly, over the phone.

☎ Reaching Out Again

• Start by making a list of geographically acceptable dealers. Call each and ask for the name of the service manager.

• Then call those managers, one by one, and have a little truth session. Tell him your name. Say you're planning to buy that make of car or truck in the next couple of weeks, and that you're trying to pick the right dealer. Tell him you think that several dealers are going to be pretty close to each other on price. But even if they're not, in the final analysis, the quality of the service department will be more important to you in the long run than saving a few hundred dollars up front, and you'd like to talk to him for a couple of minutes about his service operation.

He will like this attitude because it places the focus where he thinks it should be. It also affirms his importance in the dealership. While he runs his own show (reporting to the dealer's general manager) and produces the bulk of the dealership's profit, he probably doesn't get the respect he deserves. (Most dealer principals are sales types, as are their general managers.)

Specific Areas to Probe

• First, ask how long he's been there, and where else he's worked. (If he's just arrived, how long was the previous manager there?)

• Then, acknowledging his significant experience, ask him what he thinks may be better about his service operation than some of his same-make competitors. This will give him an open field, so to speak, and he should have some substantive things to say. If he's got a good story to tell, you may hear about how well equipped his shop is, the factory training his people get regularly, his attitude toward customers and even the dealership's overall CSI.

• If you don't hear these things, either he's shy and inarticulate or he's got no great story to tell. Give him the benefit of the doubt, and ask a few more detailed questions.

✓ **Ask about the dealership's overall CSI score, and specifically, how it stacks up against other same-make dealers in the same factory sales zone.** This is something he has to know about, given its importance to the dealer and his department's key role in making sure it's favorable. If his CSI is above average, he should be glad to tell you about it. If he hedges or says he's not sure, it's probably below average. Ask if he'd show you the report if you came in to see him. You want to buy where the CSI is at least average or better, compared to other stores in the same factory sales area.

✓ **Ask how well equipped his shop is.** Does he have to send cars out for many operations? For example, does he have wheel alignment and wheel balancing equipment? A brake lathe to turn drums (for drum brakes) and rotors (for disc brakes)?

✓ **Has the dealership won any recent factory awards for service excellence?** Do his people regularly get to go to factory training sessions (or is the boss too tight to send them)?

✓ **Does the dealer offer a courtesy shuttle service** to take customers to work or home after they drop off a car? (Many do, but few will also pick you up to return later.) Are there loaner cars or low-cost rentals? And are the service department's hours convenient for you?

Obviously, what you want to hear is that the CSI is above average for the sales zone, the service manager's job there is not a revolving door, the shop is well equipped, it wins factory excellence awards frequently, the mechanics attend factory training courses regularly, and he'd be glad to give you a shop tour, if you'd like.

After two unsuccessful attempts, beware of service managers who don't return your calls. If you have trouble getting them for a five-minute phone conversation, you may assume their customers have the same problem.

The Envelope, Please . . .

All service departments are not created equal, and you'll learn a lot from this relatively painless exercise. You should be able to pick two or three finalist dealerships near home or work. You may even come away with a sense of which dealer you'd like to buy from.

None of this means you're going to be any less disciplined in negotiating price! You're still going to work those sales operations for a minimum-profit deal. You may even use price quotes from car stores you'd never consider buying from to get concessions from your finalists. Whatever deal you strike, you'll be happier buying from the right dealer because your ongoing relationship is more likely to be a good one.

21

People who have no weaknesses are terrible; there is no way of taking advantage of them.
—Anatole France

Showtime!

You've done all your homework. You've decided either to sell your old car yourself at retail or sell it to a dealer at wholesale, and you've learned its true wholesale value. You've decided how much you can spend, and you've researched financing alternatives.

You've taken your test drives and chosen your vehicle and dealer finalists. You've got your worksheets showing dealer invoice costs, current consumer and dealer incentives, dealer holdback (if any) and carry-over allowance (for a model-year leftover).

Most important, you've got at least one alternative vehicle that's an acceptable option to your first choice, and a couple of colors you'd be happy with for each.

You're ready for the games salesmen play and the back-end add-ons they'll try to sell. You've decided whether you're a candidate for an extended warranty contract. And you've timed your "talk turkey" visits for either the end of the month or the end of a juicy dealer incentive program.

You've reviewed Chapter 4 (Psychology 101, Anatomy 101 and Reality 101) and Chapter 7 (Divide and Conquer). You've got the knowledge and the right attitude, and you're going to be a very disciplined shopper. You're just about ready.

THE GAME PLAN

Let's review what you're going to accomplish:

1. You'll visit at least three dealer finalists to negotiate a slim-profit price, using your knowledge to get a better deal than the 99.9 percent of buyers who don't have this knowledge. The car stores will understand they're competing against each other for your money, not against you. And you'll keep the price negotiation completely separate from any discussion of selling your old car or financing the new one.

However you plan to finance the vehicle, it's a good idea at the outset to give the impression that you've got an open mind about financing through the dealership, if the terms are attractive. Chances are, you'll negotiate a better purchase price if they think they have a shot at the financing profit; if they know in advance that you'll finance somewhere else or pay cash, they may hold out for a higher-profit deal. (The same thinking applies to your potential trade-in. Even if you've decided to sell it yourself, let them think initially that you'd consider selling it to them.)

2. After establishing the new-car price, you may open the discussion of financing, telling the salesman you'd like to know what the dealer or the factory has to offer so that you can compare it with other options.

3. At that time you may also open the discussion of your old car, saying that you might want to sell it to a dealer, depending on the price, and asking how much they'd pay for it. You'll also make it clear that you know what your vehicle is worth at wholesale, and that you don't plan to leave any money on the table.

WHAT SHOULD YOUR
TARGET PRICE BE FOR THE NEW CAR?

In a word, low. You're not responsible for the state of the market. But you're certainly willing to take advantage of it, like any other smart shopper.

This is not a time to be bashful about presenting lowball offers to car stores. They all won't say no. Even if they do, remember that you can always go back and offer more, but you can't go back and offer less.

Most dealers are very eager to move their inventory. They've got acres of vehicles, each costing them $75 to $150 a month in floor plan interest. They want those autos in your garage and in their service bays, where they make the real profits. Many of them might prefer making a low-profit or even a no-profit deal to making those carrying charge payments for two or three more months.

> For a domestic car in good supply with no current factory-to-dealer incentive on it, you shouldn't be reticent about starting with an offer right at dealer invoice. And you should have in mind a maximum price target, which probably should be no higher than dealer invoice cost plus 2 to 5 percent for cars listing under $20,000, and invoice cost plus 4 to 6 percent for those over $20,000.

At 2 percent over invoice a domestic dealer receives a front-end gross of $300 on a car that costs him $15,000, plus an additional $500 or so in holdback funds (3 percent of MSRP). That might not be a deal he'd love, but it's a deal thousands of car stores are making every day in the 1990s.

Import franchises used to be much tougher to deal with, but times have changed. Today even Honda dealers run ads about prices "$49 over invoice." The Honda Accord has been the best-selling car in the United States, and the best-selling cars in any country are not in short supply. Anyone who isn't buying an Accord or any other mid-priced import make for well under MSRP isn't negotiating a realistic price in today's market.

> Your maximum price target for a volume import make should be slightly higher than for a domestic, perhaps dealer invoice plus 3 to 6 percent for a car listing for $20,000 or less, and invoice plus 5 to 7 percent for those over $20,000. But we'd still start with an offer at or slightly above invoice.

If an import dealer won't talk price, move down the road to one who will. He's waiting for you, with a lot full of unsold cars.

If there's a factory-to-dealer incentive program on the car you want, you should end up with at least half of that incentive—all of it if you're buying a model-year leftover. Your offer should reflect those objectives; ask for all of it, and don't settle for less than half. If one dealer won't cooperate, take your business to another who will. In a market with several competing dealers, they shouldn't be hard to find.

Direct customer rebates should be kept out of the price negotiation. They are your entitlement, almost always paid entirely by the factory. You'll use them as part of your payment after the price is settled.

If you're shopping for a model-year leftover of a Ford or GM vehicle, you should request that the entire factory carryover allowance (5 percent of MSRP) be deducted from the price you pay. That car's value dropped like a rock the day the new models hit the dealer's lot, and 5 percent of the sticker price doesn't begin to cover the loss.

ARE THERE VEHICLES ON WHICH YOU CAN'T DEAL?

Yes. You won't get much of a price break on any car when the demand exceeds the supply. The most common example is a hot-selling new model in the first few months after its introduction. And if you must have the only teal green Accord coupe within five hundred square miles, it'll cost a lot more than those blue ones lined up on every dealer's lot.

There used to be several makes noted for holding firm on price, but they have become a vanishing breed. The European luxury cars would have liked to play the game by the old rules indefinitely, but the Japanese changed the rules. You may not get a Lexus dealer with only a two-week supply to budge much from the sticker price on an LS 400. But the Japanese invasion of their high-end turf has many of the Europeans reeling and, for a refreshing change, dealing. (For instance, a woman we know bought a BMW 535i for the price of a 525i, a model that listed for $8,000 less.)

For most of the expensive Europeans, their best sales years in this country are behind them, primarily because the Japanese are making very competitive luxury cars and selling them at more attractive prices. As BMW's design chief said in the spring of 1992, "We have no problem competing with them on technology. The big challenge is the value-price relationship."

The bottom line is that you should make aggressively low offers to just about any dealer today, even that high-flying Lexus dealer. At MSRP, the

LS 400 carries a gross profit of well over $8,000! If it's the end of the month and the cars are sitting there, he just might bite on a lower offer. (Half of $8,000 is a pretty fair front-end gross.) Remember, you can always decide to pay more.

THE OTHER CAVEAT: COMPETITIVE GEOGRAPHY

There's another factor that can severely restrict your ability to negotiate a favorable price: the number of dealers for a given make within competitive geography. If there's only one dealer for the car you want within a reasonable driving radius, he's got real pricing leverage. That's been true in the early 1990s in many markets for thinly dealered makes like Infiniti and Lexus.

GM's Saturn is a special case, where price competition is very limited because each dealer has been given an exclusive sales territory. (See Chapter 13.) Eventually, there may be three Saturn stores in your town, but they're all likely to be owned by the same person. And he's not going to compete with himself on price.

If your heart's set on a car with this dealer situation, be prepared to pay the sticker price, or possibly even more. Supply and demand is the law.

CURTAIN TIME!

Now we're going to take you through a hypothetical negotiating session. Of course, we can't script a single approach that will apply to all situations, but this example illustrates how you can use your strong base of knowledge in a very disciplined way to achieve the result you want. Think of it as a game. You've got all the tools you need to win, and dealing from strength can actually be fun.

"The Hammer, Wrapped in Velvet"

Walk into the first showroom with your worksheet pad under your arm. A salesman will greet you. (You're his "up.") He will not be happy to see your pad. If he comments on it, tell him you've got a terrible memory and might want to refer to some notes.

A note of caution: If you are female and are greeted by a saleswoman, don't assume that's a stroke of good fortune. In the research discussed in Chapter 2, dealerships seemed to steer testers to salespeople of their own gender and race, who proceeded to offer them worse deals than other testers received from people of a different gender and race. Would a nice saleswoman try to take advantage of you? You can bet on it. No matter how nice she may seem, she is assuming that you will trust her, and that your trust will lead to a higher-profit deal.

From the start, your projection should be friendly but quite confident, disciplined and firm. You are definitely someone who knows what you want, and knows a lot about what you want. (He'll quickly learn that you know more than 99.9 percent of the people who walk through the door.)

You're knowledgeable, but you're not going to be cocky about it. What you are going to be is very straightforward. And you are always going to act like someone who is going to buy a car.

Smile and introduce yourself. Then tell him that you're definitely going to buy a car in the next week or so, you've taken test drives and know exactly what you want, you're shopping several dealers, and you're going to buy where you get the best price. Then add that a friend wants to buy your old car, but you're not sure that's a good idea. Tell him you've checked out some financing alternatives, but haven't made a decision. And say that you'll be happy to discuss selling your old car to them, and to consider the dealership's financing options, but not until you've settled on the price of the new vehicle.

As an overall tactical objective, you want to be the one asking the questions, defining the key issues that need to be resolved and moving the discussion in a straight line toward a resolution. That way the pressure will be on the salesman to respond to your moves, making it difficult for him to get and keep control of the sales situation.

For example, when he begins asking personal questions about your job or marital status, it's perfectly appropriate to say, "Please don't take this the wrong way, but I know your time is valuable, and if it's okay with you I'd rather get into a discussion about the car. I already know I can qualify for financing; the question is whether we can agree on a price." If he hasn't invited you to sit in an office by this time, suggest that you go to one to discuss a possible deal in more detail.

When you get there, tell him nicely (perhaps with a little self-conscious smile, but maintaining good eye contact) that you know the auto business is supercompetitive today, and that although that makes it tougher for him you plan to take advantage of that competition, just as he would if he were you.

You should add that, frankly, you expect to buy this car for something very close to dealer invoice cost, not counting any specific direct customer incentive offer in effect, which you'd plan to use as part of the payment after you've settled on a price.

Then tell him that you also know there's a current factory-to-dealer incentive program (if there is), with payments that range from $400 to $800 depending on performance, that his store appears to be a higher-volume outlet that would earn the maximum incentive, that other similar dealers were willing to share an important part of that incentive with you, and that you assume his store would, too. *Then bite your tongue and wait for a response.* The pressure will be on him, not on you.

Remember, you're saying this very calmly, as a really nice person who just happens to be shopping in a favorable climate, from a buyer's standpoint. As long as the experts are saying this is the best time in years to buy a new car, you decided to see if it was true.

What You've Already Accomplished

You've won the first skirmish, and you've still got lots of arrows in your quiver. He can't do what he does with most prospects at this stage—find their hot button (whether they're payment buyers or trade-in allowance buyers, etc.) and move to exploit it.

You've defined the turf on which the battle will be fought: simple cash price. You've also put all the key issues on the table early in the game, making it difficult for him to waste your time bobbing and weaving around them. You are going to learn, reasonably quickly, whether these people want to sell you a car and get on to the next customer or work hard to make you a victim of Life's 80/20 Rule—the one that says 80 percent of the profits come from 20 percent of the buyers.

His Move

He's a creature of habit. He may start writing (your name, address and the details of the car you want) while he considers what to do next.

He'll check to see whether he has that car in stock. If he doesn't, tell him that other dealers told you they could work a dealer exchange for the car and wouldn't charge you anything for that.

If he has the vehicle, or one very close to it, he may ask if you'd like to take a test drive as a way to gain time to learn more about your potential weaknesses. Your answer will be, "No, thank you. I've already taken several test drives and I know what I want." Everything you do must tell him you're someone who has shopped around at other dealers and will shop around to get the best price.

Since he knows you've been shopping elsewhere, he might ask what price the other guys have quoted, or what price he has to beat. Your response, with a smile: "You know I'm not going to tell you that." (It's never a good idea to tell any salesman the prices other salesmen quote.)

He also might tell you to go out and shop around for the best price, then come back and he'll beat it. You'll say, "I'm sorry, I'm not going to spend a month playing games with car dealers. I am going to buy a car from some dealer in the next week or so. But if I can't get a serious price quote to consider on this visit, I won't be back to get one later." If he refuses, you should leave.

He won't refuse; he doesn't want you to leave. At this point he'll probably say something that moves the issue to price, the only turf you've given him. He might say, "Here's list price on the car. I'm sure we could give you a big break off that." Or he might ask what price would make you buy. Whatever he says, it'll be an opening to point the dialogue in the direction you want to go.

Your Move

Tell him that you need to move the discussion along to the real dealer cost numbers if this session is going to be productive for either of you. At this point you take out your worksheet, telling him that maybe the best place to start is with the dealer invoice cost. He'll look at your sheet and, somewhat dismayed, may say that your invoice cost numbers are wrong. Your response will be to call his bluff nicely, asking him to take out his factory invoice for the car so you can compare the numbers and see where they differ.

By now he's probably classified you as a tough customer, which is fine. (It's wrapped in velvet, but your hammer is there.) *Remember that it's much easier for you to find another dealer than for him to find another real prospect.* As long as you act like someone who's going to buy somewhere soon, he'll keep the discussion alive.

Since the salesman probably doesn't have the factory invoice and would be crucified if he showed it to you, he'll search for a way to get another person involved—his sales manager, the closer. He may do that by trying to get you to make a specific offer, one that he can take to "them" as your buddy. To shorten the agony for both of you, you should be prepared to make an opening offer, one that's well below what you're really willing to pay for the car. Here's an approach to moving the dialogue along:

Let's assume there's a current factory-to-dealer incentive program as described earlier, in the $400 to $800 range. For openers, you should offer the dealer invoice cost minus $400, or half of the maximum dealer incentive payout. Remind him that any direct consumer incentive doesn't figure into this offer, that it will simply be part of your cash payment after you settle on a price.

That offer would give the dealer a $400 profit, assuming he reaches the maximum incentive payout. And if he's a domestic or an import dealer that receives holdback, there's an additional profit of 2 to 3 percent of either dealer invoice or MSRP, depending on the make. (You shouldn't mention holdback at this juncture; save it for later, when you'll meet someone who can make a decision.)

As the salesman leaves—without the hostage deposit check you refuse to write—tell him nicely that you don't know how his store operates, but yesterday, in another dealership, they kept you waiting for long periods of time, and you're not going to do that again. If he's not back in about five minutes, you'll leave.

Also say, with due respect for his position, that if he's not someone whom you can bargain with directly to a final purchase price, without passing a lot of messages back and forth, he should bring the decision maker with him when he comes back.

As he walks away, understand that they won't buy your opening offer, whatever it is. If they did, they'd worry that you'd have buyer's remorse, wondering if you'd offered too much. You might even get cold feet, refuse to sign a deal and go down the street to another car store to see if they'd take less. So always expect them to "bump" your offer.

Don't just sit there while he's gone! To strengthen your psychological advantage, wander around the lot so that he'll have to look for you when he returns. That'll make him worry that you might leave, and it'll ensure that he won't be gone for long periods, "negotiating for you." (Remember, if he doesn't sell cars, he doesn't eat. He needs you.)

The Boss, the "Bump" and Your Hole Cards

After one or two of these round trips, the salesman will probably return with his boss, then excuse himself. The boss is likely to say that they can't sell a car at that price without losing money; they've got more invested in floor-plan interest payments than your offer allows in profit; they're not going to earn the maximum dealer incentive of $800 anyway; and the bottom line is they need another $1,000 to even consider a deal.

Your response should be that you hope that's not his best price because if it is, he's not going to sell you a car. Take out your worksheet and let him look at it.

Here's where you'll use your knowledge of holdback, if it's relevant to that make. While holdback isn't something most folks can extract from even the most desperate dealer, it can be used artfully in this game. You'll lead with your knowledge of the factory-to-dealer incentive program, then play the holdback card.

First, tell him that you're surprised that a big sales operation like his isn't at or near the maximum incentive payout two days from the end of the program, that dealers that seem to have less volume and inventory have offered to share $400 of the incentive. Say that you'd expect him to be even more eager to sell you a car if he's below the target with only two days to go.

Then point to the Dealer Holdback line on your worksheet. Say you know there's another $400 in factory holdback that's really profit for him, that if he needs another $1,000 you'll get him halfway there, that the combination of the $400 holdback and an additional $100 from you will give him another $500. And that would seem like a fair deal—dealer invoice less $300. *Then bite your tongue and wait for a response.*

If he accepts, you're probably getting close to a good deal. But don't write a deposit check or do anything to finalize it on this visit. That was too easy, and chances are, the deal can get better, either here or somewhere else. No matter what he says, there will be lots of time tomorrow to nail down a deal with him that's as good or better. Tell him you always like to sleep on big decisions, that you'll talk to him tomorrow. Ask for his business card, thank him for his time, and leave.

It's more likely that he won't accept your last offer, that he'll counter with a higher number—a much higher number. At this juncture he's expecting to start a lengthy series of concessions on both sides, to see how much higher you'll go. Don't raise your offer by more than $25, and don't do that more than twice. He'll keep that game going forever if you let him. And when you refuse to budge after two $25 raises, he may ask, "Why don't we split the difference?"

Never, ever fall for this "generous" split-the-difference offer. Instead, this is where you'll get up and say very politely that it looks as if you aren't going to agree on a price today, that you've got some other stops to make, and that your phone number is 345-6789 if he has a change of heart later.

(In fact, 99 percent of car salesmen do, 99 percent of the time.) Then ask for his business card, thank him for his time and leave. You do have other stops to make. And he will be there later if you want him.

PREPARE FOR THE MATINEE

If that was a morning show, plan a couple of afternoon performances at other dealer finalists. You'll be more comfortable in these shows, better prepared for the curve balls they'll throw because you've seen a few. By the end of the day, you'll have a good feel for the parameters of a possible deal and for the probable differences in price flexibility between dealers. Depending on the number of finalist dealers on your list, you may spend a second day completing these Round One visits.

As you review the bidding at the end of this round, factor in your feelings about where you really would like to buy. Where does that store stand on price? Whether it's on the high end or close to the leader, you'll have further discussions with the people there tomorrow.

☎ ROUND TWO

The next step can be handled best on the telephone. Call all of the players, the last ones you talked to in each store. Thank them again for their time, remind them that you're still planning to buy a new car in the next few days and that you're calling to see whether they've had a chance to think about your last offer. Your objective here is to get them down as low as they'll go for a live prospect, one they thought had got away.

They might ask, "What's the best price you've been offered?" Just say that it's well below their last offer. Whatever number they give you, tell them it's not your best offer but that you aren't going to make a decision until tomorrow, and they've got your phone number. Thank them again for their time and hang up.

Call your emotional favorite last. Start the conversation the same way. After his response, tell him that you'd really like to buy the car there, for reasons that go beyond price, but that you don't want to have to pay too dearly for the privilege. You live (or work) right nearby, and you hope he's not going to make you buy a car somewhere else.

Tell him he doesn't necessarily have to be the low bidder, but he's got to be in the ball park, and he's not quite there now. Emphasize again that you're ready to come down today and finalize the deal. *Then bite your tongue until he says something.*

If you've got two vehicles you'd be equally happy with, it's in your interest to take them both down to the wire. You might be surprised by one dealer's eleventh-hour concessions, especially near the end of a major factory-to-dealer incentive program.

Somewhere in this back-and-forth process, you'll find a deal and a dealer you can live with.

FINALIZING THE DEAL

Before leaving home, review Chapter 18 (Back-End Options: Just Say No). When you get to the dealership, make sure the car isn't loaded with dealer sticker items you don't want. If it is, demand that they throw them in free or find you a car without them.

Be alert at this stage for a host of little surprises, things salesmen "forget" to tell you about until they've got you so committed it would be a real hassle to walk away.

✓ For example, don't pay him a fee to process the documents. He can't sell anyone a car without processing documents. That's his cost of doing business, not yours.

✓ There's one surprise that advisors like *Consumer Reports* tell you to refuse—the dealer advertising charge. This charge, typically about one percent of the sticker price, is levied by the manufacturer on the dealer. It's not for his individual store's advertising but for the regional dealer advertising association.

Is this a legitimate charge to the buyer? No, and yes. On one level, it's advertising, which is his expense, not yours. (And it worked, didn't it?) But consider this question: Don't the supermarket and the gas station charge you for their advertising? Of course they do; they just don't charge you separately for it when you pay the bill. If the manufacturers were brave enough to build this mandatory dealer charge into their invoice costs, there'd be nothing to debate. Since they aren't, we can understand why a dealer might try to pass it along.

The best way to handle this surprise is to tell him that his competitor isn't charging you for it. He may not want to risk losing the sale over it. And if all dealers want to charge for advertising, tell them the one that doesn't charge gets the sale.

You may end up paying it anyway. If you do, try to use the concession to get one in return, like a set of deluxe carpet mats thrown in at no charge.

✓ If you want the extended warranty contract, make sure you understand what it covers and what the deductibles are, and confirm that it's guaranteed by the manufacturer. (Read all the fine print.) Then offer *half* of the asking price, and don't pay more than two thirds. *Although you don't have to buy it when you purchase the car, they want to sell it then, and you'll never have as much bargaining leverage as you do when they think this could make or break the whole deal.*

✓ Read every word of the sales agreement before you sign it. Make sure all the blanks are filled in. And be sure someone with proper authority signs it for the dealership before you do. (If the salesman's signature isn't binding, you don't have a firm deal.)

✓ This is the time to explore the potential appeal of the financing plans offered by the dealer. You've done your homework, so you've got a basis for comparison.

✓ This is also the time to say you're not sure it's smart to sell a used car to a friend. If the price were fair, you'd consider selling it to them. (Don't give them an asking price; make them give you a price first. And don't accompany them for the inspection show pantomime.) They'll take your car and come back with an offer, which you can counter based on the homework you've done on the car's true wholesale value. If they won't pay you that number, or something close to it, take it to one of those places that will. End of negotiations!

Unfortunately, buyers are not really wise on leasing right now. . . . If you are willing to pay $250 a month, I can make a lot of money on you. If you haven't compared me with other dealers on the details, I can probably really take advantage of you . . . if I were that kind of guy.

—General manager of a
large import-make
dealership
(printed in *Kiplinger's
Personal Finance Magazine*,
August 1991)

22

The Leasing Alternative: Breaking the Language Barrier

The 1990s may come to be known as the Decade of the Auto Lease. Pick up any paper. Half the car ads are pushing leases, and not just at the luxury end of the spectrum, where leased vehicles have traditionally accounted for over half of new-car sales. What's happening?

What's happening is that sales have been so depressed for the last few years that many manufacturers have decided that, short term, they would rather lose money than lose market share. So they're digging into their pockets to underwrite leases, "buying down" the interest rates to lure buyers with lower monthly payments. These subsidized rates have been down to 2.7 percent and lower. (Audi was so desperate to move cars, it offered a 0 percent lease rate in 1991.)

The automakers may be losing their shirts on these cut-rate lease deals, but they're moving metal. In response to attractive low-payment lease offers, individuals leased over 1.3 million vehicles in 1991, compared to only 250,000 in 1982. Retail and commercial leasing combined account for over 15 percent of total auto sales, and that number is increasing by more than one percentage point a year. Some analysts predict that leasing will represent more than one third of new-car and -truck sales by the late 1990s. That would make about 22,000 auto dealers very happy.

WHY DEALERS LOVE LEASING

Leasing is popular among dealers for several reasons, all of which have to do with profit.

• First, it generates quicker customer returns to the dealership, since the average lease term of about three years is shorter than the average new-car loan of four or five years.

• Leasing also provides them with a predictable supply of relatively low-mileage, one-owner cars—the bread and butter of a profitable used-car operation.

• *Most important, leasing frequently gives them an opportunity to make more profit than they'd earn on a straight sale of the same vehicle.* That's because most consumers don't understand leasing well enough to negotiate the terms effectively.

We'll help you solve that problem. But the first question to address is whether leasing represents a viable option for you. Let's examine the issues you should consider.

THE PLACE TO LOOK IS IN THE MIRROR

Leasing can make a lot of sense for some people and be a poor choice for others. Start by asking yourself these questions:

• Do you like to trade cars reasonably frequently, at least every three or four years?

- Do you value the image you project by always driving a late-model vehicle?
- Would you like to drive a more expensive car than you can afford to buy?
- Do you drive an average of less than 15,000 miles a year?
- Would you rather take the cash you'd use for a down payment and put it into an investment that appreciates?
- Conversely, are you someone who can afford to make the monthly payments but doesn't have enough cash for a significant down payment?
- Are you more intrigued with the concept of paying only for vehicle usage than with the psychic rewards some people get from vehicle ownership?
- Are you willing to make monthly car payments indefinitely?
- Do you own a business that will be making those payments?

If you answered yes to most of these, you're a candidate for leasing. Leasing is a viable option for people who trade often and drive a moderate number of miles each year, especially if they can write off most of the payments as a business expense.

If you answered no to most of these initial questions, ask yourself a few more:

- Do you hate making car payments?
- Do you look forward to Car Payment Freedom Day, when you've made your last payment and you get the title certificate from the lender?
- Do you buy new cars infrequently, typically keeping them five years or more?
- Are you someone who likes to squeeze the last drop of value from every dollar you spend?
- Is keeping up with the Joneses relatively unimportant to you?
- Are you someone for whom pride of ownership of a car or truck is important?
- Do you drive significantly more than 15,000 miles a year?
- Do you have enough cash to make a down payment of 20 percent or more on the vehicle you want?

If you answered yes to most of these and no to most of the previous group, you're not a good candidate for leasing.

If you are a candidate for leasing, you'll be pleased to know that in many cases, manufacturers' subsidies may enable you to lease a better car than you could buy with the same monthly payment, and do it with little or no down payment.

If you're not a candidate for leasing, you'll take comfort in this headline from a 1991 Mercedes-Benz ad: "The average 1984 car lost 69% of its value in the first five years." While a 69 percent loss is nothing to brag about, it does say that the average car retained 31 percent of its value after five years . . . which is 31 percent more value than you'll ever retain if you always lease your cars.

The only way to squeeze every drop of value from the money you spend on a car is to drive it until the wheels fall off. If you pay for a car in four years and use it for eight years, you'll be driving relatively cheap transportation during the last half of its life. And you'll spend much less for the use of a car than someone who leases several vehicles sequentially over the same period.

On the downside, you'll pay the psychic cost of driving a somewhat older car than your less frugal neighbors, the Joneses.

If you're considering leasing, pay close attention to this next point.

AUTO LEASE ADS ARE FINE PRINT HEAVEN

Let the buyer beware; mouse type was invented for car leases. You'll need a magnifying glass to read the ads, and you'd better use one. Here are some actual fine print examples (the italics are ours):

- "Lease based on total MSRP including destination charge."
- "Optional equipment not included in monthly payment."
- "Mileage charge of $.15 per mile over 15,000 miles/year."
- "Monthly payment based on *10% down payment.*"
- "Customer responsible at signing for first monthly payment, insurance, taxes, title and registration fees, *plus $450 documentation fee.*"
- "Prices may vary based on dealer contribution."
- $7,079 *dealer/customer* capitalized cost reduction due at lease signing."
- "*$350 disposition fee due at lease end if vehicle is returned.*"
- "Non-refundable prepaid rental reduction of $1,350 (cap reduction) required."

If leases seem more complex than standard auto loans, it's primarily because the language of leasing is so different from that of buying. And both new-car dealers and independent leasing companies can use that extra layer of "boomfog" to take advantage of leasing prospects.

LEASING BASICS, DEMYSTIFIED

If you like the idea of leasing but are put off by the language barrier, relax. Although leasing has more aspects to consider than conventional financing, it is neither mysterious nor hard to understand. A straightforward walk through the basics should convince you that it's a relatively simple concept that gets tangled in its own underwear by the terminology.

The Simple Concept   Think of leasing as long-term car rental. When you sign a lease, you agree to make a specific monthly payment for a specific number of months in return for use of the car during that period. In lease language, you are the lessee, and the company that leases you the car is the lessor. The lessor is typically not a dealer, but a separate company that buys the car from a dealer and then leases it to you. This could be one of hundreds of independent leasing companies or an auto manufacturer's captive finance subsidiary, such as GMAC or Toyota Motor Credit Corporation.

What You Pay For   The monthly payments you make to the leasing company cover two basic elements:

• First, you're paying them for the estimated depreciation in the vehicle's value over the term of your lease. You're not buying the whole car; you're paying only for the part of its value that you use. That's why the monthly payment will be lower than a standard auto loan payment.

• Second, you're paying them a lease rate, the rough equivalent of a bank's interest charges on an auto loan. That rate covers three things: (1) their interest payments on the car for the time you have it, (2) their other costs of doing business and (3) their profit.

In the language of leasing, the amount of depreciation that you pay for is determined by the difference between two components: the capitalized cost and the residual value. Here's the simple equation:

Depreciation = capitalized cost minus residual value

• The capitalized cost is the purchase price, the amount the leasing company pays (or says it pays) to buy the car. It can also include other miscellaneous start-up charges, title and registration fees and sales taxes, if you choose to fold them into the lease and pay for them monthly instead of up front.

• The residual value is an estimate of the car's average wholesale value at the end of the lease period. It is almost always stated as a percentage of the vehicle's original sticker price (MSRP), and that percentage typically is established by the bank or other financing source.

If you think about this for more than five seconds, you'll recognize that the higher the capitalized cost and the lower the residual value, the more depreciation you'll pay for and the higher your payments will be. And, of course, vice versa. (Hold this little revelation in the back of your mind for a few minutes.)

The lease rate is the finance charge by which the leasing company makes most of its money. The higher the lease rate, the higher the payment. And, of course, vice versa. (Save this flash of brilliance with the previous one; we'll return to both after we've covered a few more bases.)

Keep It Closed   Most leases are closed-end agreements, which is the only kind you should consider. At the end of the lease term, you return the car and walk away with no additional obligation. The residual value of the vehicle is predetermined; if the car is worth less, that's the lessor's problem, not yours, as long as you've taken reasonably good care of it.

Keep It Repaired   Because the residual value estimate assumes you'll return the car in good shape, you'll pay the cost of fixing anything beyond normal wear and tear. The better leases contain guidelines for acceptable damage, but the definitions can be fuzzy. To be safe, assume that "unacceptable damage" means anything you'd repair or replace if you owned the vehicle. (A dented fender. A broken antenna. An automatic window that won't go down.)

Down Payments   One of the selling points of a lease is that you don't need to come up with a down payment. With many leases, you'll get the keys in exchange for a check covering the first month's payment, the first year's license fees and taxes, a lease initiation charge and a refundable security deposit equal to one month's payment.

But there are lots of exceptions, especially in the most attractive leases. You'll note that the ads for many of those subsidized, low-payment lease deals have fine print that says something like: "Estimated monthly payment is based on Suggested Retail Price, with a non-refundable prepaid 10% capital cost reduction"—otherwise known as *a down payment.* Another ad might say, "Assumes dealer capitalized cost reduction of $3,124," or "Dealer participation may affect actual cost," indicating that dealers are sharing the cost of the subsidies with the manufacturers by reducing the purchase price.

Whether it comes from you or the dealer or both, the "cap reduction" acts as a down payment that pays part of your total obligation in advance, reducing the amount of your monthly payment.

With or without a subsidized lease rate, it could be smart to make a down payment, perhaps using the proceeds from selling or trading in your old car. That "investment" might give you a nice return, reducing your monthly installments enough to cut your total outlay over the term of the lease.

The Purchase Option   You'll usually have the option to purchase the vehicle for its residual value at the end of the lease term. If the purchase option price is higher than this, the residual value is set too low, which means they're trying to stick you for more depreciation than they really project. Our advice: Assume you're smelling a rat, and find another leasing company.

Excess Mileage Charges   The lease contract will specify a mileage allowance and a penalty for exceeding it. Typical terms: 15,000 miles a year over the term of the lease, and a penalty of 15¢ per excess mile. If you know you'll exceed the limits, some lessors will sell you extra miles at the beginning of the term for a somewhat lower rate, and you'll pay for them with a somewhat higher monthly payment.

Since the terms of most leases are negotiable, you may find you can get the lessor to waive the mileage restriction, reduce the penalty charge or increase the yearly mileage allowance.

The Lease Term, Early Terminations and Insurance Gaps   What's the best lease term for most people? One that's no longer than the length of the original bumper-to-bumper factory warranty, so you'll never have to face a big repair bill.

Don't sign a lease for a term that's longer than you're sure you'll keep the car. Every lease has an early termination clause, and it's a painful end to consider. You'll usually have to make all of the remaining payments. (No leasing company will let itself get stuck with a year-old car from a three-year lease contract. The big depreciation hit occurs in that first year, and one year of payments doesn't begin to cover it.)

Be sure to ask what happens if the car is stolen or totaled in a wreck. This could become a big financial problem for you with some lessors. All lessors treat a stolen or wrecked car as a form of early termination. Your insurance company pays them the car's market value, but that number can be a lot lower than the amount you still owe on the lease. With most leasing companies, you are responsible for the difference.

These companies may advise you to purchase additional gap insurance to cover this contingency. Dealers and leasing companies will be happy to sell it to you—for an arm and a leg. One large independent leasing company quoted a $100 per month premium on a five-year lease of a luxury car. Clearly, the biggest gap here is between the price and the value of this insurance.

There is some good news: This gap is not a problem if you lease from a few manufacturers' captive finance companies.

In July 1991, GMAC began shielding its customers from losses if a vehicle leased from them is stolen or wrecked, paying any difference between the insurance payoff and the lease balance, and allowing the customer to get a new car. To cover potential losses, they provide their own gap insurance, either by self-insuring or by paying a modest premium for each vehicle leased (probably under $50 per vehicle). Yes, they build this cost into your monthly payment, but it's a lot less than you'd pay for individual coverage.

As of mid-1992, GMAC, Ford Motor Credit Corporation and Nissan Motors Acceptance Corporation included this automatic gap insurance in their leases. But the captive finance operations of the other Big Six auto manufacturers—Toyota, Chrysler and Honda—did not provide this built-in coverage. As retail leasing grows in importance, it's likely they are going to have to follow suit to remain competitive.

Before you sign any lease, be sure to ask how the lessor would handle this total loss situation. If there's no built-in gap insurance, treat it as a bargaining point and ask them to provide it at no cost. Tell them you know at least three big leasing companies that will be happy to include it for you. It's not smart to leave yourself open to this financial risk.

These Lemons Don't Make Lemonade   All states have lemon laws, which protect consumers from getting stuck with chronically ill cars. And most of these laws give the lessee (you) the same rights as the lessor.

But why should you have to go through that hassle, when it's the leasing company's lemon? They buy all those cars, so they've got the leverage with dealers and manufacturers. Ask how they'd handle a lemon situation. If you like their answer, get it in writing. If you don't, lease from someone else.

The Nickels and Dimes Add Up   Oh, those miscellaneous charges! There's usually a *lease initiation fee* of around $250—extra revenue for the lessor, who may even share it with the selling dealer, depending on how high they can set the purchase price. (If the lessor helps establish a high-profit purchase price, such as the sticker price, the dealer might share some of that profit with him.)

Then, when you turn in the car, there's often a *disposition fee* of several hundred dollars—more extra revenue for the lessor.

Assume that these kinds of charges are negotiable, and tell the lessor you'll lease from the company with the lowest miscellaneous numbers.

Yes, you'll pay vehicle title and registration fees and state and local sales taxes on a leased vehicle. You may pay them separately or have them included in the monthly payment, amortized over the term of the lease. Some states will tax you on the full capitalized cost; others will exclude the residual value. And if your state has a *personal property tax*, expect the leasing company to add that in, too.

IS LEASING MORE EXPENSIVE THAN BUYING WITH CONVENTIONAL FINANCING?

A lot of people think it is. A lot of the time they're right—for three basic reasons:

1. Since a car depreciates more rapidly in the first two or three years than in the balance of its life, lessees are always paying for the most expensive depreciation years. But buyers get to average all the years as they pay off a loan and continue to drive a car that's paid for.

2. Dealers probably get a higher average purchase price for a leased car than for a straight sale. That's because many lessees aren't savvy enough to discover the real purchase price on a lease . . . and to negotiate a more favorable one.

3. When you lease, you've got an extra mouth to feed: the lessor. Instead of paying interest to a financing institution, you pay it to a leasing company at a higher lease rate, which includes the interest they pay to buy the car, plus factors to cover their costs and a profit.

You must also recognize that you can't expect the leasing company to negotiate a rock-bottom purchase price with the dealer and then pass the savings on to you. Instead, they'll want to establish a higher purchase price for your lease and pocket the difference as profit. And, of course, a higher purchase price (a.k.a. capitalized cost) means higher finance charges, a higher monthly payment and more revenue for the leasing company.

Despite these factors, leasing frequently beats buying-and-financing in today's competitive market, where manufacturer-subsidized programs can be too good to turn down. Here's how to analyze the details of one of those special leasing offers and determine whether it represents a better deal than a straight purchase:

Running the Numbers: Leasing vs. Buying

Let's assume a $15,000 purchase price, whether leasing or buying.

Conventional Financing: Assume you can put 20 percent down ($3,000) and finance the balance of $12,000 for three years at an annual percentage rate of 10 percent. Using the amortization table on page 42, you determine that your 36 monthly payments will be $387.24 each, totaling $13,941. Adding your $3,000 down payment, the total cost of the car will be $16,941.

The Special Leasing Offer: Under the manufacturer-subsidized lease in this example, there's no down payment and the monthly payment is only $249. Three years' payments come to $8,964, and you can buy the car at the end of the lease for a preset residual value of $6,917. Total outlay: $15,881, or $1,060 less than the conventional financed-purchase option.

There's also a significant cash flow advantage to this lease. Since no down payment is required, you can invest the $3,000 down payment you would have made for a conventional purchase, earning interest on it over the three-year lease period. Further, your monthly lease payment will be $138.24 lower than the conventional purchase payment, giving you an additional $4,977 to invest over that 36 months. If you simply put that down payment and the difference in monthly payments into a savings account paying only 4 percent after taxes, you'll have an additional $650 to $700 at the end of the lease period.

Conclusion: Although miscellaneous lease charges (security deposit, initiation and disposition fees) would reduce the advantage, leasing with the purchase option beats buying and financing in this specific example. In a different example, with less favorable lease terms, you might find that a conventional purchase beats leasing.

LEASING: THE MASTER JUGGLER'S TURF

Because the key elements of leasing sound like a foreign language to most people, the salesmen at dealerships and independent leasing companies can use that language barrier as a screen for some of the most profitable deals in the auto business. They are the industry's master jugglers, and most buyers can't follow all the balls because they don't even understand what their names mean.

As you know now, three major factors determine the size of your monthly lease payment:

• The length of the term of the lease.

• The projected depreciation while you have the car, which is determined by the difference between the capitalized cost (the purchase price) and the residual value (the estimated wholesale value at the end of the lease).

• The lease rate, the leasing company's finance charge, which covers their cost of money to pay for the car, other business costs and profit.

Of course, the jugglers don't want to discuss the details of any of these individual elements. Usually, they don't have to; most customers don't even know the questions to ask. As soon as a prospect mentions leasing, the only thing leasing jugglers want to talk about is the monthly payment. And because the monthly payment on a terrible leasing deal can be a lot lower than one on a good purchase deal, it's relatively easy for them to fleece the uninformed.

IF YOU DON'T KNOW THE DETAILS, YOU DON'T KNOW ENOUGH

To avoid overpaying for a lease, you must focus on the details, just as you would if you were buying and financing the vehicle. Unfortunately, the legal requirements of a lease agreement differ from those of an auto loan; often a lease does not have to disclose the relevant details, such as the capitalized cost and the lease rate. If a dealer or leasing company refuses to disclose this information, you may assume that they've got something to hide. Walk away and lease from someone else; plenty of leasing operators will deal fairly with knowledgeable shoppers.

Here are some suggestions on how to go about negotiating a favorable lease:

RULE 1: TO GET A GREAT LEASE, DON'T MENTION LEASING . . . YET

Remember that flash of brilliance you've been saving? (The higher the capitalized cost, the more depreciation you'll pay for, and the higher your payments will be.) Now's the time to use it, taking the right first step to negotiate the lowest possible capitalized cost.

When you walk in and tell a salesman you want to lease a car, you give him an unfair advantage. Resist that temptation, and you'll give yourself an advantage.

As soon as he knows you're there to lease, he'll do everything he can to focus on the monthly payment and to avoid other subjects. *The main thing he doesn't want you to focus on is the purchase price (otherwise known as the capitalized cost) because the higher the purchase price, the more money he makes.*

The dealer doesn't want to negotiate the selling price of a leased car. He wants the capitalized cost to be the full sticker price, or some other number that's a lot higher than you'd be able to negotiate if you were buying instead of leasing. (The same is true if you're dealing only with a leasing company. They'll try to set a capitalized cost that's much higher than the price they paid for the car. So don't even enter a leasing office without knowing the realistic purchase price in advance.)

How do you resolve this dilemma? By not getting into it. When you walk in, don't mention leasing. As far as that salesman is concerned, you're there to buy that car, and you're going to buy it where you get the best price. Your job at this stage is to negotiate a great price for a straight purchase, just as you would if you'd never considered leasing. You're going to use your knowledge of the dealer invoice cost, factory-to-dealer incentives and holdback, if appropriate. You're also going to be sure they reduce the purchase price by the amount of any direct consumer rebate in effect. *And you're not going to utter the L-word until you've got a firm purchase price.*

Here's how this back-door approach could fatten your wallet. Assume that you end up with a capitalized cost $2,000 lower than you'd get without using this tactic. With an 11 percent lease rate and a three-year term, your monthly lease payments would be $65.48 lower, saving you $2,357.

Once you've established a firm price—one management has agreed to—tell the salesman you want to lease the vehicle. Say that you want a closed-end lease, specify the term length and tell him what capital reduction (down payment) you're prepared to make, if any.

He may act surprised. He may even balk at the news, telling you there's no way they can lease it at that price, perhaps even saying that leases are always based on the sticker price. (He's disappointed because he missed the big-margin sale he often gets from uninformed lease prospects. Your response will show that you're not one of them.)

You'll tell him that you're very familiar with leasing—that leasing has nothing to do with the purchase price, it's just an alternative way to finance a new vehicle. You know the dealer is going to sell the car to a leasing company, which will lease it to you. And if he's willing to sell it to you for that negotiated price, he'll sell it to anyone for that price.

You'll also say that you're aware the dealer will collect a fee from the leasing company (either an independent or the manufacturer's captive finance company) for steering the transaction their way.

Then you'll tell him that if his store isn't willing to proceed with negotiating the other terms of the lease based on the agreed purchase price, you're sure you can find another, more cooperative dealership. Just as with a straight purchase, you must be willing to end any lease negotiation abruptly if you think a salesman is being unreasonable. (Remember Reality 101: You can walk away from any deal and be absolutely certain there is one just like it, and probably better, around the next corner.)

Chances are, they won't let you walk after spending that much time getting to a purchase price. You're a live sale for them!

RULE 2: DON'T LET THEM ROB PETER TO PAY PAUL

Just as a buyer can have a great purchase price wiped out by a lousy trade-in allowance, a lessee can negotiate a great capitalized cost and have it offset by a residual value that's too low and/or a lease rate that's too high. It's the old shell game, and let the buyer beware.

- You need to know all the other details, starting with the residual value. (Remember: The lower the residual value, the more depreciation you'll pay for and the higher your payments will be, and vice versa.) This value is stated as a percentage of the vehicle's original sticker price (MSRP). The number is established by the financing entity. As you probably know, different vehicles depreciate at different rates, depending on the demand for them as used vehicles. Your monthly lease payment could be significantly lower for a more expensive car that holds its value better than for a less expensive car that depreciates quickly.

It's also common for different financing entities to assign different residual values to the same vehicle. When leasing began to grow dramatically, many banks and finance companies lost a lot of money guessing wrong on residual values. As a result, some lenders estimate more conservatively than others. That could cost you money if your leasing company works with the wrong lender.

For example, assume you're considering a three-year lease of a sedan with a sticker price of $20,000. One financing source estimates a 55 percent residual value of $11,000; another uses 48 percent in its calculation, or $9,600. You will pay that $1,400 difference—an extra $38.88 per month.

Tell the salesman that you are aware of these potential differences. You understand that the residual percentage may not be negotiable at any specific financial institution, but you expect him to check several sources to determine which is the most favorable.

You have a right to know the residual value number being used. It should be a realistic estimate, not a managed number put there to get more money from you. If it's below the purchase option price listed in your closed-end lease agreement, that indicates they're charging you for more depreciation than they project. It also indicates you should find another leasing deal if they won't change their residual value estimate.

- The other detail you need to examine is the lease rate. (This is the other insight you've been saving: The higher the lease rate, the higher the payment, and vice versa.)

Neither the lessor nor the dealer will want to disclose this rate to you, and there's no law that says they must. But if they won't tell you, assume they've got something to hide and find another leasing arrangement. Expect them to get more cooperative as they see you prepare to leave.

The salesman may try to hide behind the lease language barrier, telling you that "the money factor is .00467." Don't be intimidated by this. Take out your calculator and multiply .00467 by 24 to come up with the lease rate of 11.2 percent. (This is the equivalent of a bank's annual percentage rate, or APR, on a loan.) If that 11.2 percent lease rate is a lot higher than the current rates you've found for conventional auto loans, you shouldn't buy it. Ask the salesman to check the rates of other leasing companies. (Each dealer typically works with several.) If he refuses, tell him you're going to talk with some other dealers who will and leave.

RULE 3: AVOID THE DOUBLE WHAMMY; LEASE EARLY IN THE MODEL YEAR

Timing can be as important in leasing as in buying, and the right time to lease is early in each model year. You'll usually get a better lease deal then, for two key reasons:

• First, most auto manufacturers have at least one midyear price increase. If you lease after the increase, you'll have a higher capitalized cost, which will mean a higher monthly payment.

• Second, the later it gets in the model year, the closer you'll come to leasing a car that will be four years old in only 36 months. The bank will establish a lower residual value at the outset, which will require a higher monthly payment to cover four years of depreciation in three years.

So if it's July, August or September, it probably will pay to wait until October, November or December and lease next year's model.

RULE 4: MAKE THEM COMPETE FOR YOUR BUSINESS

When you lease a car, three different organizations have a financial interest in the transaction: the dealer that sells the car, the leasing company that buys it and leases it to you, and the financing entity that provides the money for the purchase. In a business with these kinds of interrelation-ships, the team members have a common interest in taking care of each other's wallets.

Unfortunately, none of them has any real interest in taking care of *your* wallet. The higher the bill, the more money each makes. So you can't count on the leasing company to negotiate a slim-profit purchase price with the dealer; you can't count on the dealer to try to beat down the leasing company's "money factor"; and you can't count on either of them to pressure the financing institution to raise its residual value estimate or lower its cost of funds. Everyone rubs everyone else's back, and you pay each masseuse.

How do you deal with this? The same way you would if you were buying the vehicle—by pitting one leasing team against another and discovering which one wants your business the most. To shop smart, you must get specific offers, including all the details, from at least two dealers and a couple of independent leasing companies—the bigger, the better. Assume that all lease deals are negotiable . . . and shoppable.

Dealers have a compelling reason to close every lease deal they can: higher customer retention. Research shows that about 80 percent of leasing customers return to the same store when they're in the market for their next vehicle. That's more than double the percentage of regular purchasers who return to the same dealerships. This simple fact will give leasing prospects increasing leverage throughout the 1990s, as leasing's share of sales continues to rise.

RULE 5: UNDERSTAND THAT FACTORY-SUBSIDIZED LEASES ARE HARD TO BEAT

This rule frequently invalidates Rules 1, 2 and 3.

Manufacturers that decide to move cars with subsidized leases tend to make the terms too good to turn down. Here's how they do it:

- First, they get the dealer to share the burden by making a substantial "contribution to capitalized cost reduction"—a cut in the purchase price, so that you're not faced with a lease deal based on the sticker price of the car. (You'll see the amount of this "contribution" in the fine print of the ads promoting these offers.)

- Then they keep the monthly payments at attractive below-market levels by having their captive finance subsidiaries manipulate the lease rates and/or the predetermined residual values. As an example, in 1991 Cadillac inflated the residual value estimate on a vehicle by about 10 percent to reduce the monthly payments. And in the fall of 1992, in an all-out effort to replace the Honda Accord as America's best-selling car, Ford offered a two-year Taurus lease with no money down and an annual lease rate of just 0.5 percent (compared to 8 percent for standard two-year leases on other models).

The net result is usually a lease that you can't beat anywhere, with perhaps one exception: at another dealership for the same make. (That's why Rule 5 doesn't invalidate Rule 4.)

If you remember only one thing from this book, it should be, *Make them compete for your business.* Some dealers are always going to be more desperate than others.

It always pays to shop around. Even on an appealing factory-subsidized lease, don't assume that the terms in the ad are as rigid as they seem. Contact several dealers for that make and tell them you're going to lease where you get the best deal. One dealer might make additional concessions to get your business; maybe he'll lower the purchase price another $500, or waive the mileage limitation, or reduce or eliminate the down payment.

RULE 6: BEWARE OF THE LOWBALL LEASE OFFER

The lowball opener has found its way to the leasing side of the business. Whenever you see a "no money down, only $179 a month" offer, read the fine print. You may find that it's for a stripped-down model no one would want. The purpose, of course, is to get you into the showroom, where they'll move you to a more profitable model—one with much higher payments.

RULE 7: READ THE FINE PRINT
—ALL OF IT—BEFORE YOU SIGN ANYTHING

If the lessor won't give you a copy to study, there's a reason—one good enough for you to find another, more cooperative lessor.

23

There is no substitute for hard work.
　　　　　—Thomas Alva Edison

We won't say Edison was wrong. But, considering all the better mousetraps he invented, surely he knew there was more than one way to catch a mouse.

There Must

Be an

Easier Way!

The problem with doing something right is that somebody's got to do it. We recognize that many of you are sitting there now feeling that this task will require more time and effort than you can give it, wondering if there aren't easier ways to accomplish the objective. You may even be wishing that someone else could do it for you.

As you might expect, we think you should practice what we preach. We're convinced that you can negotiate the best deal yourself, using the methods outlined in this book.

But yes, there are easier ways to buy new cars and trucks. And we wouldn't be providing a comprehensive service if we didn't mention them. Here are four alternatives to consider:

EASIER WAY #1—CARBARGAINS

If you like the idea of having someone else do the hard part (negotiating for you), there's a special service you should know about. It's called CarBargains, and it's offered by the Center for the Study of Services (CSS), a nonprofit consumer service organization in Washington, D.C. (As noted in Chapter 15, CSS publishes *CarDeals*, our source of detailed information on manufacturers' current consumer and dealer incentive programs.)

CarBargains is a systematic process in which CSS gets dealers in your market to bid competitively against each other to sell you the car you want. Here's how it works:

1. You call CarBargains toll-free at (800) 475-7283 and tell them the make, model and style of car or truck you wish to buy. They'll charge your credit card $135 for the service.

2. Within two weeks, they will get at least five dealers in your area—including any specific dealers you request—to bid blind against each other for your business. Each dealer commits to a selling price that's a specific dollar amount above or below the factory invoice price.

The participating dealers know that they're in a competition, and that it will take a low bid to win. They also know that CarBargains has a real customer, since anyone who has paid for this service is almost certain to buy a vehicle very soon from one of them.

The Center for the Study of Services has helped thousands of people save money on new cars and trucks via competitive bidding. As you'd expect, they use their solid base of inside information to remind dealers of current factors that give them room to cut prices. Factory-to-dealer incentive programs, manufacturers' holdback and year-end carryover allowances could all come into play in the bidding, depending on each dealer's specific sales and inventory situation. This is also a house sale for the dealer, with no salesman's commission to pay.

3. When the bids are in, they'll send you a report containing a specific price quote sheet for each dealer, showing exactly how far above or below the invoice cost the dealer has agreed to sell the vehicle. The report also includes the name of the sales manager responsible for this commitment. Each dealer's bid must include all the costs involved, including any advertising association fees, processing fees or other miscellaneous charges. You'll have no last-minute surprises.

Their report will also include a printout showing the dealer invoice price for the base vehicle and for all factory-installed options and equipment packages. You'll be able to add the invoice prices for the vehicle and the options you want, then add (or subtract) the amount of the dealer's agreed markup (or markdown). Thus, you'll know the price you'll pay before you leave home.

4. You'll visit one or more of the dealerships, select the car you want and see the sales manager listed on the quote sheet to purchase the car at the price the dealer has already agreed to. The bidding dealers will honor their commitments; they know they won't get future opportunities to bid if they don't. (*Important note*: The Center for the Study of Services has no ties to specific dealers. The only income they derive from the bidding process comes from the consumers who order the service.)

CSS believes that CarBargains frequently results in "the lowest price a dealer will allow," simply because he perceives their phone call as a one-shot, out-of-the-blue opportunity for an incremental sale that he wouldn't normally get.

This strikes us as an attractive, reasonably priced alternative for people who just can't negotiate for themselves. Indeed, CarBargains may be a worthwhile $135 card for any buyer to play. An attractive bid from a relatively unattractive dealership might improve your bargaining leverage with the dealer down the street.

In the next two easier ways, you'll do the negotiating, but you won't have to do it in person.

EASIER WAY #2—THE HOUSE SALE VIA TELEPHONE AUCTION

In this approach, you phone your dealer finalists to get bids. (Think of this as your own version of CarBargains.) Ask to speak to the fleet sales manager, not to a salesman. If they don't have a fleet manager (some stores don't), or if the fleet manager deals only with customers buying more than one vehicle, ask for the sales manager. Be sure to write down his name.

When you speak to him, tell him what car (make, model and style) you're in the market for, and that you're going to buy it from some dealer within the next week. Say that you're calling several dealers' fleet sales managers, just once each, to get bids on the car. You'll buy wherever you get the best price, and you aren't going to share one dealer's bid with another. Tell him you know this will be a house sale, meaning there will be no salesperson's commission involved. If it's true, add that you've never talked to any salesman at his store.

Then tell him you've done your homework, and you've got a good fix on what that car will really cost the dealer. You're aware of the factory invoice cost and holdback, as well as any factory-to-dealer incentive programs in effect. You understand that the decision on sharing the dealer incentive is theirs to make, but you're getting bids from other dealers, and you'd expect that the lowest bidder will be sharing a good portion of it.

Next, tell him that to be able to compare apples to apples you're asking each dealership to bid against the factory invoice price. You want to know how much above or below invoice they will charge for the vehicle you want.

You'll ask him about all the charges on the invoice so that you'll know who's including what. Is the destination charge there? How much is it? A dealer advertising association fee? Dealer preparation charges? Will they show you the actual invoice for the car you buy?

Ask whether there are any other charges you'll have to pay that aren't on the factory invoice, saying you won't buy from a dealer that springs a last-minute surprise. Tell him to exclude any customer rebate from the bid. And ask whether they'll honor their bid if they have to exchange cars with another dealer to get the exact one you want.

In sum, what you want from each dealer is a commitment to a number over or under the invoice price, plus a full disclosure of any other costs they will charge for the car you want. If you don't get straight answers from one dealer, call others.

Why don't we favor this less painful approach? Many dealers refuse to give serious bids over the phone to individuals because they feel they'd be wasting time with window shoppers. As you know, they want to get you on their turf, in the showroom, where they feel they'll have the advantage.

Frankly, we believe your physical presence as a knowledgeable, disciplined shopper helps establish you as a more serious, more real prospect—one they're more likely to spend time with and, ultimately, make more concessions to.

But some dealers will do business over the phone, and many people might handle this telephone auction approach very successfully.

EASIER WAY #3—THE "HOUSE SALE" VIA MAIL AUCTION

This is a similar approach, with the U.S. Postal Service replacing the phone company on the initial sales contact. First you call the finalist dealerships and get the name of the fleet sales manager and the store's mailing address. Then you mail each sales manager the same letter, requesting that he bid on the car you want.

Your letter will state what you'd say on the phone in Easier Way #2, except that you don't have to spend time establishing the house sale idea. To enhance your chances of being taken seriously as a well-informed prospect, you'll attach a copy of your worksheet. The letter will contain your name and address, as well as your home and work phone numbers. (They are probably more likely to respond by phone than by mail.)

This approach requires a little more advance planning, especially to enable you to take advantage of favorable timing for a factory-to-dealer incentive promotion.

We believe that if you mail six of these letters, you should get two to four interested responses.

EASIER WAY #4—AUTOMOBILE BROKERS

These days many consumers are buying cars and trucks through automobile brokers. These people charge you a fee for their service—frequently (if you can believe it) as little as $50 or $100. They negotiate to get a price that's supposed to be much lower than you could get, since they move a lot of metal for dealers.

There are two issues to examine here:

• One is that he's likely to buy your car from a dealer in Timbuktu, which is not exactly on your way to anywhere, especially when you need service. He'll say, "Your local Chevy dealer will service it; it's done all the time." As you know, we don't think that's the ideal situation.

• Beyond service, there are the questions of how cheap the broker's services really are and how much he really saves you. Let's consider the low service fee. How do the numbers work for him? Assume he charges $100 a car. Remember, he's got to communicate with you, negotiate with one or more dealers, and coordinate the paperwork and delivery, which he frequently makes himself. All this for only $100?

Assume he sells a car every working day, about 250 a year, giving him a gross income of $25,000, before phone bills. No way, José! Assume he sells two a day, 500 a year, giving him a $50,000 gross. Maybe, but it still seems a little skimpy for the work involved.

Clearly, many of these brokers get a significant portion of their income from the spread between what they pay the dealer and what they charge you. This leaves open the question of how much they really save knowledgeable, disciplined shoppers, who might negotiate equally good or better deals on their own.

As one broker reported in a May 1991 issue of *Automotive News*, he "sells" 300 to 500 vehicles in an average year, and makes "anywhere from $70 or $80 to more than $1,000 per transaction, depending on the vehicle *and the deal he can cut with a dealer*." And while all brokers contacted said they always pass along any factory-to-consumer incentives, the factory-to-dealer incentives are a different story. As one put it, "We don't get too involved with the dealer's business, we [just] supply them with the audience."

We'd suggest using a measure of caution when dealing with brokers, to avoid simply trading one car salesman for another. It's certainly in the broker's interest to maximize his profit on the deal. And one of the easiest ways for him to do that is to have an alliance with the dealer that increases his spread as the overall profit increases.

Some of our sources tell us these kickback alliances are common, that many buyers can expect surprises like unwanted add-on options—for example, dealer-applied paint sealant that "lists for $750 but will cost you only $225" (and probably costs the dealer only $50).

In sum, you must draw your own conclusions about these hired guns. Maybe some of them are terrific and others are not. Overall, we'd bet that you can negotiate a better deal yourself, if you're willing to put in the effort.

Even if you're not, we believe that an alternative like CarBargains is likely to save you more money than any broker. Why? Chances are that broker is dealing with only one dealer for each make. (Concentrating his business is the main reason he can get good prices, right?) That means, by definition, there's little or no price competition between dealers for your business. And in the retail auto business it's the competitive aspect that enables a buyer to take advantage of price flexibility, which may change dramatically from dealer to dealer . . . and from week to week.

The same principle applies to those fleet purchase referral services that are offered by all kinds of affinity groups. They all claim they'll set you up with a nearby participating dealer whose fleet manager will give you a terrific price.

The problem: He's typically not competing against any other fleet manager. That dealer paid for the privilege of being on that referral list. He doesn't want to compete with anyone for your purchase, which means that you will usually pay for the privilege of buying from him.

The solution: If you use one of these referral services, you should ask for at least three different dealer referrals within your driving radius. And make sure each fleet manager knows he's in a competition.

If we've said it once . . . whether you're negotiating for yourself or having someone else do it for you, the key to getting the best deal will always be having several dealers compete against each other for your business.

The buyer needs a hundred eyes,
the seller not one.
　　　　　　　—George Herbert

24

Resisting
the Final
Temptation

Now comes the fun part: uninhibited emotional involvement without financial risk! Driving that new baby home . . . Being seen by envious friends and neighbors . . . Inhaling that new-car smell . . .

Not so fast! There's one more piece of unfinished business, some work to do now to avoid a potential pile of grief next week: *the inspection. Smart buyers allow at least one extra day at this juncture to ensure that they'll be happy with the car they drive home.*

WHAT YOU DON'T SEE IS WHAT YOU'LL GET

That new car or truck belongs to the dealer until the minute you pay him, sign the delivery receipt and drive the front wheels off the lot. If it's got any problems, they're going to get fixed much quicker while he still owns it, before you've given them the final check. (Once you drive away, they can claim that any defect happened after you took delivery.)

Prepare the salesman in advance: Tell him that when the car is ready, you plan to inspect it carefully, and that you'll expect them to correct any problems before you take final delivery. Tell him to be sure to leave the dealer's tags on the car because you want to test-drive it while they still own it. That message should motivate the dealer to pay even closer attention to his checklist for the car before you get there.

MAKE THIS A DAY GAME ... ON A NICE DAY

You can't inspect a new vehicle properly in the dark or in the rain. Put the trip off until you can do it in broad daylight on a reasonably nice day. Take a friend or relative to help; four eyes and ears are better than two.

Here are the things your inspection trip should cover:

1. Check the odometer. If it shows more than about 300 miles, they'd better have a good explanation. (Maybe they made an exchange with a dealer 200 miles away. But maybe they're trying to slip you a demonstrator that someone's been driving for a few weeks.)

2. Make sure all the optional equipment you ordered is on the car. Then have the salesman take you through the operation of all the equipment—the air conditioner, cruise control, lights, sliding sunroof, stereo system (the basics only for now), electric windows, washer-wipers, remote side mirrors and remote fuel cap opener ... everything. Make sure it all works. (Incidentally, this is part of his job.)

3. While you're checking equipment, use your accomplice to help check all the lights—the turn signals, backup lights and brake lights, dome light and other interior lighting, even the glove compartment, trunk and engine light (if there is one). Ask whether the manufacturer has set the interior lights to go on briefly when you leave the car at night and, if so, how long they stay on.

4. Go over the interior fabric areas very carefully. On cloth areas, make sure the fit is perfect everywhere, and there are no stains or tears.

Ditto for the carpets and the headliner (it's that cloth or plastic covering between your head and the roof), which should show no sloppy glue stains.

5. Pay close attention to the exterior finish, both body and chrome. It should be perfect, without scratches or dents. (New-car owners should be allowed to put the first "dings" in their own doors.)

If there are small scratches, they can buff them out reasonably easily. *But if the scratches are long enough and deep enough to require repainting, you should refuse the car, period!* The original factory finish is very difficult for even the best body shop to match, and partial-panel matching is next to impossible. They'd probably end up repainting the whole side or panel to fix a small imperfection, and chances are, you'd be unhappy with the result.

6. Check for previous body damage. It's rare with new cars, but it happens—on test drives or in transporting dealer exchanges. Look for mismatched paint on adjacent body parts or ripples in the surface. (Federal law says the buyer must be given a disclosure statement on previous damage.)

7. Check the fit and finish on all things that open and close— windows, passenger doors, hood, trunk, glove box. And make sure all the tires match.

8. While the hood is up, ask the salesman to show you where all the fluids go and how to use the dipsticks to check the levels. The engine oil. The brake fluid. The automatic transmission fluid. The power steering fluid. The radiator anti-freeze, and even the windshield washing solution. If any of these is not at the proper level, either the dealer has done a poor job of prepping the car or there's a leak.

9. Most important, take it for a test drive, ideally while the dealer's tags are still on the car, not with temporary or permanent tags assigned to you. That way it's still under his insurance coverage, and he can't claim you've taken delivery.

Drive the car reasonably aggressively to test it. If it's an automatic transmission, do the gears seem to shift smoothly and at natural progression points? Does the cruise control work?

Accelerate to about 30 mph on a straight, flat, dry road with little or no traffic, and take your hands off the wheel. If the vehicle pulls left or right, it may have alignment problems. Slam on the brakes. Does it stop squarely? And find a road with some bumps to drive over to see if there are any annoying squeaks and rattles.

Carry a pad and make a list. Give it to the dealer to copy (keep the original yourself), and tell him you'll come back after they call to say they've fixed everything. At that time you'll examine it again and, if it's perfect, you'll turn over the final check, sign the delivery receipt and drive it off into the sunset. They won't love you for all this, but you will.

10. One last important detail: **Be sure you've communicated with your insurance agent,** so that you're covered the moment the front wheels hit the street in front of the dealership.

We cannot tell a lie; this chapter is a commercial.

- *It's for something you'll need.*
- *At $19.95, it's a fine value.*
- *It comes with a money-back guarantee.*
- *You can order it toll-free anytime.*
- *And, if you find this book valuable, you'll want it.*

25

Call

1-800-288-1134

I f you're going to shop smart for that new car or truck, you'll need current information on three key elements:

• The state of the automobile market. (We call it the Big Picture in Chapter 3.)

• The actual dealer invoice price for the specific vehicle or vehicles you're interested in buying.

• Details of the manufacturer incentive offers in effect, both the consumer rebate and financing offers *and* the factory-to-dealer cash incentives that are normally not publicized.

You don't have to buy this information from us, but, frankly, you ought to buy it from somebody. And we know of no other source that has put together a package this complete, priced it as a "best buy" value, supported it with a money-back guarantee and given you an 800 number to make it easy to order.

Ask yourself this question: Since the average new car is going to cost more than $17,000, shouldn't you spend $19.95 first for a way to get through the process and come out knowing that you did not overpay? (Think of it as a down payment on feeling good about that purchase.) Here's what that $19.95 buys:

1. THE BIG PICTURE

Take another look at Chapter 3. The first piece of the Fighting Chance package is the current month's version of the Big Picture chart on page 169 of the Appendix, along with our analysis of what it means for shoppers. You'll see each make's sales performance and general inventory status, compared to the total market, through the most recent month available. With this information, you'll be able to judge which makes might be more flexible on price in the specific sales environment you will encounter.

In addition, we will provide any important new information that we feel might impact your purchase decision—information that becomes available between the periodic editions of this book. (For example, this could include significant changes in basic warranty protection that might affect your purchase of an extended warranty policy. And, as the model year is winding down, we'll inform you of any carryover allowances announced by the domestic makes. For model years after 1993, we'll also include a revised list of models that are "family relations," like the one on pages 49–50 in Chapter 11.) We know of no other new vehicle pricing service that provides this kind of current insight.

2. *CARDEALS*—THE AUTHORITATIVE REPORT ON CURRENT INCENTIVE PROGRAMS

The second piece of the Fighting Chance information package is the current issue of *CarDeals*, the report on manufacturers' incentives that's shown on pages 172–182 of the Appendix. This report is updated every two weeks by the Center for the Study of Services, a nonprofit consumer service organization. It outlines details of the manufacturer incentive offers in effect—both the consumer rebate and financing offers and the factory-to-dealer cash incentives. *CarDeals* is a very valuable tool for car shoppers and an important piece of our information package. No other pricing service includes it.

3. COMPLETE DEALER INVOICE PRICE DATA

For each car or truck, you'll get the pricing for all the configurations the manufacturer offers. That way you'll be able to make price/value comparisons between different trim levels. (Remember, a higher trim level often represents a better value because it includes standard equipment in the base price that would be extra-cost items in a lower trim level.)

Our $19.95 package price includes this dealer invoice price data for one vehicle. Pricing information for additional vehicles costs $5 each.

But Wait, There's More

When you order a vehicle printout from us, you'll frequently get a second one free: the previous price for that same vehicle.

Many manufacturers increase prices during the model year, sometimes more than once. (For instance, Ford introduced the 1991 Explorer in early 1990 and increased its sticker price in September 1990, February 1991, April 1991 and June 1991!) As price increases occur, it is common to find identical vehicles on dealers' lots with different sticker prices, reflecting the different invoice prices that were in effect when they purchased the vehicles.

In that situation, it is to your advantage to know the different dealer invoice prices for each vehicle. That's why, if there has been a model-year price increase, we'll send you two complete sets of pricing data—the most recent price and the price that immediately preceded it. (The manufacturer's effective date is shown in the upper-right corner.)

Here's another bonus: If you're shopping early in the model year and are trying to decide whether to buy the new model or one of last year's leftovers, at your request we'll include the final dealer invoice price for last year's model along with the printout for the new one.

We know of no other new-vehicle pricing service that provides either of these additional price printouts. And we believe they can be powerful bargaining tools.

When we created Fighting Chance, our objective was to offer a service that was demonstrably better than the existing alternatives. Here's an overview of three major competitors:

The _Consumer Reports_ Auto Pricing Service   The most well-known, and probably the largest, auto pricing service is the one offered by _Consumer Reports_. They charge $11 for a printout for one car, $20 for two, $27 for three and $5 for each additional car. While this sounds reasonable, they frequently treat each different bodystyle and trim level combination as a separate printout. In contrast, our printouts cover all the configurations a manufacturer offers for a given vehicle, making it more efficient for shoppers to compare the relative values.

For instance, Ford offered the 1992 Explorer in 2-door and 4-door bodystyles for both 2-wheel-drive and 4-wheel-drive models. To compare all the models, you would have needed four printouts from _Consumer Reports,_ costing $32.

Although we believe our printouts are a better value, we have great respect for the service _Consumer Reports_ provides in each issue. Indeed, the April annual auto issue is an excellent source of information on vehicle safety, reliability, comfort, convenience and economy.

The AAA's Auto Pricing Service   The national AAA organization has a new-vehicle pricing service which you access by calling either a 900 number (at $1.95 per minute) or an 800 number (where they bill your credit card $11.95 for one vehicle, $19.95 for two). You must tell them the year, make, model and trim level of the vehicles you want, as well as the major factory-installed options. They give the total dealer invoice and sticker prices over the phone and mail you a printout. Each local AAA club is an independent affiliate of the national organization. Some clubs market the national service to members, while others have their own versions.

Our 1991 experience with the national club's service and one large local club's version was not reassuring. We ordered 1991 Ford Explorer pricing and received outdated information from both.

• The national AAA's printout dated September 6, 1991, listed Ford's price as of April 2, but Ford had increased the 1991 Explorer price on June 7. Members were still receiving the old price three months later.

• The local affiliate's printout dated October 24, 1991, gave the Explorer's price as of February 8, ignoring the _two_ subsequent price increases of April 2 and June 7.

Members using this information may have been put on the defensive by salesmen telling them it was old data. (They had no way to check whether the pricing they received was current.) While these may be aberrations in an otherwise spotless record, they suggest to us that AAA's suppliers may not be diligent about updating their databases and that the clubs may not be able to monitor their performance effectively.

You should also be aware that many AAA affiliates have a deep-seated reluctance to upset the retail automotive establishment. In several states the club's board of directors is either headed by or populated by—you guessed it—car dealers. If you live in one of those states, don't expect your local club to give you strong ammunition to do battle with its board members.

We value the AAA highly in its major areas of expertise: emergency road service and, in many states, insurance and travel services. But we believe there are superior alternatives to its national and local new-car pricing services. Fighting Chance is among them.

Auto Pricing Books   Several publishers do a credible job of compiling new-car pricing data. You'll find their paperbacks in bookstores and on newsstands for about $5 a copy. The problem with these sources isn't accuracy, it's timeliness. For example, Edmund publishes three editions for domestic cars (in November, January and May) and two for import makes (in February and June). If there hasn't been a price increase or two, they're fine. But every major Japanese make raised prices significantly in March 1992—too late to make February's book and too early for June's. Also, with the model year starting October 1, many people can't wait for these books to hit the shelves; they want the information *now*. That's what they get from Fighting Chance.

The Fighting Chance information package is easy to order: Just dial 1-800-288-1134, 24 hours a day, 7 days a week. We fill and mail all orders no later than the next business day.

The price of the complete Fighting Chance information package is $19.95, plus $3 for shipping and handling, and it includes dealer invoice pricing for one vehicle. Pricing for additional vehicles is $5 each if you request them with your initial order. You may charge the purchase to Visa or MasterCard. (If you live in California, we must add the sales tax of 8.25 percent.) If you'd rather mail a check, you should make it payable to Fighting Chance, 5318 East 2nd Street, No. 242, Long Beach, CA 90803.

Our information package comes with a money-back guarantee. If you are not satisfied, for any reason, just mail the original report back to us within 30 days, along with a brief note telling us the reason, and we will refund the total amount you paid, either crediting your charge card or sending you a check, depending on your original method of payment.

Education is what you have left over after you have forgotten everything you have learned.

—Anonymous

26

The Executive Summary

Our objective is to make this guidebook the most comprehensive and useful information package available to people shopping for new vehicles. While it would be impossible to compress it into a pocket-size checklist, we have tried to highlight below the major points covered, for use as a memory trigger as you go through the shopping and negotiating process.

✓ **For openers, have a current overview of the automobile busi-**

ness. What's the sales and inventory picture for the vehicles you're shopping? The poorer the sales and the higher the inventories, the better the deal is likely to be. (Chapter 3)

✓ **Adjust your attitude.** Project total emotional detachment around car salesmen. ("A car is a car.") Be ready to walk out if you don't like what's happening. Remember, there's always a deal that's as good or better around the next corner. They need you much more than you need them. (Chapter 4)

✓ **Watch all three ways the car store can make money on you:** (1) the price you pay for the new car, (2) the financing and other back-end add-ons they try to sell, most of which are of little value, and (3) the real price they pay for your trade-in vehicle. (Chapter 5)

✓ **Develop a smart buyer's plan.** Learn what your current car is really worth at wholesale and retail. Decide whether you'll trade it or sell it yourself. Shop for money before you shop for cars. Visit car stores to narrow your choices. Gather information on dealer costs. Understand the overall state of the automobile market, including current consumer and dealer incentive offers. Do some homework to choose your dealer finalists. Make timing work for you. Put all the pieces together to approach car stores with an aggressive offer. Play them off against each other to maximize your leverage. And resolve to let them do the stewing. (Chapter 6)

✓ **If you're going to trade, keep the discussion of the price you pay for the new car separate from the discussion of the price they pay for your current car.** (Chapter 7)

✓ **Learn the true wholesale value of your current car before you talk with any car salesman about a trade-in.** (Chapter 8) And sell it yourself if you expect to get top dollar for it. (Chapter 9)

✓ **Deal with the key financing issues before you deal with the dealer.** Shop smart for money, to provide a basis for determining if the dealer's financing proposal is attractive. (Chapter 10)

✓ **Make your tire-kicking and test-driving visits "away games," if you can.** And try to retain two or three equally attractive vehicle alternatives, perhaps by exploring "family relations." (Chapter 11)

✓ **Consider the "Disappearing Car Company" and "Disappearing Dealer" factors as you narrow your choices.** (Chapter 12) And remember that those new one-price, "no-dicker" dealers may change their prices frequently. (Chapter 14)

✓ **Learn everything you can about what those vehicles really cost the dealer.** Bone up on dealer invoice prices, factory-to-dealer incentives, dealer holdback and year-end carryover allowances. Make a worksheet showing all the elements. (Chapters 15 and 16)

✓ **Make timing work for you.** Try to buy at the end of a dealer incentive program. And in general, gather data early in the month, but negotiate price at the end of the month. (Chapter 16)

✓ **Be prepared for the unexpected, both the games salesmen play and the high-profit options they'll try to sell as add-ons.** (Chapters 17 and 18) And determine beforehand if you're a candidate for an extended warranty contract. (Chapter 19)

✓ **Pick your dealer finalists based primarily on service considerations and geography, not price.** Research this issue by talking to service managers, not car salesmen. (Chapter 20)

✓ **Approach the negotiating sessions in a disciplined, confident manner, using your now-considerable knowledge base as a lever to keep control of the discussion.** Set a maximum price target of dealer invoice plus 2 to 5 percent for mid-priced domestics, invoice plus 3 to 6 percent for mid-priced imports, but start much lower (at dealer invoice if there are no current factory-to-dealer incentive programs). (Chapters 21, 15 and 16)

✓ **Aim to get at least half of any dealer cash incentive and all of any year-end carryover allowance.** (Of course, you'll get all of any direct customer incentives, such as factory rebates.) To strengthen your leverage, remind dealers of holdback profits they'll receive later, if appropriate. (Chapters 21, 15 and 16)

✓ **Above all, don't be too eager to make a quick deal.** Nobody's first offer will be his best. Play two or three dealers off against each other, using the phone for follow-up negotiations with your dealer finalists. The secret to winning: Make it competitive every step of the way. (Chapter 21)

✓ **If you're considering leasing, ask yourself the right questions to determine whether it makes sense for you, learn the language, follow the rules in Chapter 22 and read the fine print before you sign anything.**

✓ **If this all seems like more than you can handle, check Chapter 23 for easier ways, particularly the CarBargains option.**

✓ **Be sure to give that car or truck an inspection that would make** a marine colonel proud before you give the salesman the final check and sign the delivery receipt. (Chapter 24)

✓ Prepare yourself to bargain effectively for the vehicle you want by having (a) a current overview of the market, (b) up-to-date dealer invoice pricing for the vehicle, including the previous price if there has been an increase, and (c) a list of current incentive activity, including factory-to-dealer cash incentives. You may obtain this information directly from us by calling Fighting Chance at 1-800-288-1134, or you may obtain it elsewhere. But be sure to have it. (See ordering details in Chapter 25.)

Appendix

THE BIG PICTURE

This Model Year vs. Last Model Year
(Based on Hypothetical 5 Months' Results)

	Brand Sales Performance Compared to Total Market			General Brand Inventory Levels*	
	Cars	Trucks**	Total	Cars	Trucks**
Total Market	**– 6%**	**+ 6%**	**– 2%**	**Average**	**High**
Acura	Above avg.	—		High	—
Alfa Romeo	Poor	—		High	—
Audi	Below avg.	—		Very high	—
BMW	Above avg.	—		Average	—
Buick	Above avg.	—		Average	—
Cadillac	Average	—		Average	—
Chevrolet/Geo	Below avg.	Below avg.		Average	High
Chrysler	Above avg.	Above avg.		High	Average
Dodge	Average	Excellent		Average	Average
Eagle	Above avg.	—		Very high	—
Ford	Above avg.	Above avg.		Average	Average
GMC	—	Average		—	High
Honda	Average	—		Average	—
Hyundai	Poor	—		High	—
Infiniti	Above avg.	—		Average	—
Isuzu	Average	Poor		Very high	Very high
Jaguar	Poor	—		Average	—
Jeep	—	Excellent		—	Average
Lexus	Excellent	—		Low	—
Lincoln	Poor	—		Average	—
Mazda	Average	Poor		High	High
Mercedes-Benz	Below avg.	—		Average	—
Mercury	Above avg.	—		Below avg.	—
Mitsubishi	Above avg.	Poor		High	Very high
Nissan	Above avg.	Average		High	Average
Oldsmobile	Poor	Above avg.		Very high	Average
Plymouth	Poor	Above avg.		High	Average
Pontiac	Average	Above avg.		Average	Average
Porsche	Poor	—		High	—
Range Rover	—	Below avg.		—	Average
Saab	Average	—		Average	—
Saturn	Excellent	—		Low	—
Subaru	Poor	—		Very high	—
Suzuki	Above avg.	Average		Very high	Very high
Toyota	Excellent	Below avg.		Low	Average
Volkswagen	Poor	Poor		Very high	High
Volvo	Below avg.	—		High	—

*Total market inventories tend to fluctuate between a two-month and a three-month supply. General brand classifications are assigned subjectively, based on an overall assessment of how levels compare to the average range.

**Truck category includes pickup trucks, minivans, full-size vans and sport-utility vehicles.

1993 ALL-AMERICAN SPEEDSTER

(effective 2/10/93)

FACTORY CODE NO.	MODEL/TRIM LEVEL	DEALER INVOICE	RETAIL (MSRP)
S88	AAA 4-Door Wagon	$15,700	$18,400
S87	AA 4-Door Wagon	$13,000	$15,200
S86	A 4-Door Wagon	$12,800	$15,000
S85	AAA 4-Door Sedan	$14,300	$16,800
S84	AA 4-Door Sedan	$12,200	$14,300
S83	AA 4-Door Sedan	$11,900	$13,900

STANDARD EQUIPMENT BY TRIM LEVEL

A trim level:

Driver side airbag
Power front disc brakes/rear drum brakes
Dual power mirrors
Digital clock
3.0-liter V6 EFI engine
Full wheel covers
Fuel cap tether
Lights for ashtray, door courtesy, trunk,
  glove box, under hood, headlight
  switch, cargo area, dome

AM/FM radio w/4 speakers
Split bench seats w/ dual recliners;
  65/35 split fold-down rear (wagon)
Power steering
Map pockets
P205/70R14 SBR all-season tires
  (blackwall)
Tinted glass
Cloth upholstery
Luggage rack for wagon

AA trim level (in addition to or in place of A trim level):

Deluxe cloth upholstery
Diagnostic warning lights
Remote release, decklid/liftgate

Paint stripe
Cast aluminum wheels

AAA trim level (in addition to or in place of AA trim level):

Air conditioning
Convenience kit
Illuminated entry system
Reclining front bucket seats w/6-way
  power driver seat & lumbar supports
P205/65R15 SBR blackwall tires

Full console w/armrest & storage
3.8-liter V6 EFI engine
Automatic on/off/delay headlights
Speed-sensitive power steering
Tachometer
Luxury cloth upholstery

PREFERRED EQUIPMENT PACKAGES

FACTORY CODE NO.	MODEL/TRIM LEVEL	DEALER INVOICE	RETAIL (MSRP)
444B	AA	$1,500	$1,800

Includes 725 manual air conditioning; 757 rear window defroster; 211 f&r floor mats; 129 power door locks; 888 AM/FM stereo radio w/cassette; 254 cruise control; 343 power windows; 298 power driver seat; 765 P205/65R15 tires. Prices reflect discounts of $600 dealer invoice and $730 suggested retail.

1993 ALL-AMERICAN SPEEDSTER

EQUIPMENT & ACCESSORIES

FACTORY CODE NO.	ITEM	MODEL/TRIM LEVEL	DEALER INVOICE	RETAIL (MSRP)
291	Passenger airbag	All	$400	$500
725	Manual air conditioning	A, AA	$700	$850
735	Automatic air conditioning	AAA	$150	$190
525	Anti-lock brakes	All	$500	$600
754	Cargo cover	Wagons	$ 60	$ 75
254	Cruise control	All	$190	$225
757	Rear window defroster	All	$140	$170
129	Power door locks	A, AA	$210	$250
222	California emissions	All	$ 75	$110
947	3.8-liter V6 EFI engine	AA, AAA	$470	$560
143	Engine block heater	All	$ 20	$ 30
211	Front & rear floor mats	All	$ 40	$ 50
888	AM/FM stereo+cassette	All	$140	$175
861	High-level audio system	All	$250	$300
	(Includes controls for bass, treble, balance, fade; seek-scan tuning; AM stereo; Dolby noise reduction; 80 watts power)			
862	Compact disc player	All	$400	$500
	(Includes cassette; requires 861 high-level audio system)			
311	Power moonroof	AAA	$700	$800
	(Requires 725 manual air conditioning when 735 automatic air conditioning is not ordered)			
298	6-way power driver seat	AA	$250	$300
299	Dual 6-way power seats	AAA	$250	$300
314	Rear-facing third seat	Wagons	$130	$160
301	Leather bucket seats with	AA	$500	$600
	console	AAA	$400	$500
524	Leather steering wheel	AAA	$ 65	$ 90
	(Requires 254 cruise control)			
343	Power windows	A, AA	$300	$360
106	Rear window washer/wiper	Wagons	$100	$150
	(Requires 757 rear window defroster)			
765	P205/65R15 blackwall tires	AA	$130	$150
608	Conventional spare tire	All	$ 60	$ 75
	(Replaces rear-facing third seat on wagons)			
Destination Charges		All	$500	$500

Note: This chart contains fictitious information about a vehicle and a manufacturer that do not exist. It was created solely as an aid in helping the reader learn to build a new-vehicle worksheet, as illustrated in Chapter 15.

Volume 2, Number 16 August 7, 1992

CARDEALS

Rebate and Incentive Programs Currently Offered on New Cars and Light Trucks

A Newsletter Published by the Center for the Study of Sevices/Consumers' CHECKBOOK
806 15th Street, N.W., Suite 925, Washington, DC 20005 (202) 347-7283

This is information on deals being offered by car manufacturers as of August 7, 1992.

Manufacturers sometimes offer *customer* rebates directly to the consumer. You can get the rebate as a check in the mail or you can have the dealer credit the rebate immediately as a discount to reduce the price of your car. A dealer will tell you if any *customer* rebates are available, so you don't have to worry about missing out on something you are entitled to.

Another type of deal offered by car makers is factory-to-*dealer* cash incentive programs. In these programs, the manufacturer gives the dealer a cash payment for every car the dealer sells. Manufacturers sometimes advertise these factory-to-dealer cash incentive programs, but often the programs are secret.

Dealers don't have to tell you about factory-to-dealer cash incentive programs, and a dealer doesn't have to give you any part of the cash incentive payment it receives for selling you a car. Dealers may use these payments for advertising, employee rewards, extra profit, or in other ways. It's up to you to get the dealer to pass all or part of the cash incentive payment along to you. The information this report gives you about on-going factory-to-dealer cash incentive programs will enable you to negotiate with the dealer.

Here are some tips on using the *CarDeals* information—

• If you are considering several makes/models of cars that seem roughly comparable in value-for-the-dollar, be sure to check whether one carries a rebate or cash incentive program that will significantly drop its cost. It's not unusual for the maker of one car to be offering no rebate or incentive program while the maker of a similar car is offering a rebate worth $1,000 or more. That $1,000 may be just what it takes to make the second type of car the best choice for you.

• If a car you want doesn't currently carry any special deals, consider waiting. New programs start all the time.

- To get all or part of the factory-to-dealer cash incentive money that a dealer will receive for selling you a car, you may have to negotiate. Let dealers know that you are aware of the money and that you intend to shop several dealers until you find one that gives you some or all of this factory-supplied cash.

- Some factory-to-dealer cash incentive programs give dealers larger payments per car as the dealers sell more cars during the program period. Unless otherwise noted, when you see a range in our listing (say, $400–$800), this means that a dealer gets more cash if it sells more cars. In some programs, all dealers have the same volume targets. In such programs, you can expect large dealerships to get larger cash payments than small dealers, because the large dealers sell more cars. In other programs, larger dealerships have to meet higher volume targets in order to qualify for cash than small dealers have to meet, so there's no reason for you to expect to get a better deal at a large dealership. In our listing, we tell you the programs where incentive payments are "based on sales targets set for the dealer," rather than targets that are the same for all dealers.

- In programs that give dealers higher incentive payments as the volume of cars sold increases, you might do well to delay your purchase until nearly the end of the program period so that some dealers are likely to be at the highest cash incentive plateau.

- If the car you want is part of an incentive program in which payments go up as sales volume goes up, be sure to shop at several dealerships in hopes of finding one that is at the highest payment level.

- In some programs, a dealer that meets a sales target gets extra cash for all cars sold earlier in a period, before it met the target. Since meeting its target may get the dealer hundreds of dollars for each previously sold car, the dealer might give dramatic discounts as it gets close to its target.

- Although you can get a *customer* rebate in the form of a check from the manufacturer, you may be better off to have the dealer credit the rebate as a discount to reduce the price of your car; in some states, doing so will reduce your sales tax.

- Some manufacturers offer reduced-rate financing plans as an alternative to a customer cash rebate. These plans are noted in our listing. You must decide whether the rebate or the finance plan is better for you. The answer depends on the size of the rebate, the factory-offered plan's Annual Percentage Rate (APR), the APRs available from other lenders, the amount you'll be borrowing, and how long a period you'll be borrowing for. On a 48-month loan, each percentage point you cut your APR is the equivalent of a car price discount of about $18.50 per $1,000 of loan.

To illustrate, assume you could get a $13,000, 48-month loan from a bank at a 12 percent APR, and that the special factory plan's rate is 7.9 percent. The savings from using the factory plan would be estimated as follows: (12 *minus* 7.9) *times* 13 *times* $18.50 = $986.

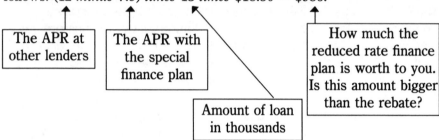

The APR at other lenders

The APR with the special finance plan

Amount of loan in thousands

How much the reduced rate finance plan is worth to you. Is this amount bigger than the rebate?

The table on the following pages shows factory-to-customer rebates (followed by a "C") and factory-to-dealer cash incentives (followed by a "D"). The deals apply to 1991 and 1992 vehicles. The programs run through the date shown in the column marked "End." For information on deals on other car types and programs that have ended, or on specific regions, call 202-783-3001.

Model	Cash to Customer (C) or Dealer (D) and/or Finance Plan (plans below)	End
SUBCOMPACTS		
Dodge Colt '91/'92 (3-dr)	$700 (C) or Plan 2 (except residents CA, HI)	8/31
Eagle Summit '91/'92 (3-dr)	$700 (C) or Plan 2 (except residents CA, HI)	8/31
Eagle Summit '91/'92 (4-dr)	$1,000 (C) or Plan 2	8/31
Eagle Summit '91/'92 (wagon)	$500 (C) or Plan 2	8/31
Ford Escort '91	$750 (C) or Plan 4 and 5% of list price (D)	9/23
Ford Escort '93 (except wagon and LX 4-dr)	$400–$500 (C) (varies by region) or Plan 4; and 5% of list price (D) plus $0–$180 (D)** based on sales targets set for individual dealer	9/23
Ford Escort '92 (wagon)	$400–$1,000 (C) (varies by region) or Plan 4; and 5% of list price (D) plus $0–$180 (D)** based on sales targets set for individual dealer	9/23
Ford Escort '92 (LX 4-dr)	$400–$750 (C) (varies by region) or Plan 4 and 5% of list price (D) plus $0–$180 (D)** based on sales targets set for individual dealer	9/23
Ford Escort '93 (Standard 5-Spd and LX 5-Spd)	$400 (C) or Plan 4	9/23
Ford Escort '93 (Standard auto and LX auto)	$200 (C) or Plan 4	9/23
Ford Festiva '91	$1,000 (C) or Plan 4 and 5% of list price (D)	9/23
Ford Festiva '92	$1,000 (C) or Plan 4	9/23
Ford Festiva '93	$500 (C) or Plan 4	9/23
Geo Metro '92 (5-Spd except convertible)	$500 (C) or Plan 5	9/23
Geo Metro '92 (auto except convertible)	$700 (C) or Plan 5	9/23
Geo Metro '92 (convertible)	$1,000 (C) or Plan 5	9/23
Geo Prizm '92	$1,500 (C) or Plan 5	9/23
Honda Civic '92 (4-dr)	$400 (D)	9/2
Hyundai Elantra '92	$1,000 (C)	10/2
Hyundai Elantra '92 (GL 5-Spd base)	$750 (C)	10/2
Hyundai Excel '91	$1,200 (C)	10/2
Hyundai Excel '92 (4-dr L)	$750 (C)	10/2
Hyundai Excel '92 (except 4-dr L)	$500 (C)	10/2
Mazda Protegé '92	$1,400 (C)	9/8
Mercury Tracer '91	$750 (C) or Plan 4 and 5% of list price (D)	9/23
Mercury Tracer '92 (wagon and base model)	$400–$1,000 (C) (varies by region) or Plan 4	9/23
Mercury Tracer '92 (LTS)	$400–$500 (C) (varies by region) or Plan 4	9/23
Mercury Tracer '93 (4-dr and wagon)	$200 (C) or Plan 4; and free air conditioning	9/23
Nissan Sentra '92 (except w/F09 package)	$1,000 (D)	9/2
Nissan Sentra '92 (w/F09 package)	$1,000–$1,843 (D) (varies by region)	9/2
Plymouth Colt '91/'92 (3-dr)	$700 (C) or Plan 2 (except residents CA, HI)	8/31
Subaru Loyale '92 (AWD wagon)	$800 (D)	11/3
		(continued)

Model	Cash to Customer (C) or Dealer (D) and/or Finance Plan (plans below)	End
SUBCOMPACTS (cont.)		
Suzuki Swift '92 GT	$1,000 (D) or (C)	10/2
Suzuki Swift '92 (3-dr GA, 3-dr LE)	$500 (D) or (C)	10/2
Suzuki Swift '92 (4-dr GA, 4-dr GS)	$500 (D) or (C)	10/2
Suzuki Swift '93 (3-dr GA)	$300 (D) or (C)	10/2
Suzuki Swift '93 (4-dr GA, 4-dr GS)	$300 (D) or (C)	10/2
Toyota Corolla '92	$800–$1,000 (D) based on sales targets set for individual dealer	9/2
Toyota Tercel '91/'92	$200–$400 (D) based on sales targets set for individual dealer	9/2
COMPACT CARS		
Acura Integra '92	$500 (D)	9/2
Buick Skylark '92	$500–$1,250 (C) or Plan 3 ($500 w/package SA or SB; $750 w/package SC; $1,000 w/package SD or SM; $1,250 w/package SE or SF)	9/23
Chevrolet Cavalier '92	$750 (C) or Plan 5	9/23
Chevrolet Corsica '92	$500 (C) or Plan 5	9/23
Chrysler LeBaron '92/'93 (coupe)	$1,500 (C) or Plan 2	8/31
Chrysler LeBaron '92/'93 (sedan and convertible)	$1,000 (C) or Plan 2	8/31
Dodge Shadow '91/'92	$700 (C) or Plan 2	8/31
Dodge Spirit '91/'92	$1,000 (C) or Plan 2	8/31
Ford Tempo '91	$400 (C) or Plan 4 and 5% of list price (D)	9/23
Ford Tempo '92	$500 (C) or Plan 4	9/23
Honda Accord '92	$500 (D)	9/2
Mazda 626 '92	$1,200 (C)	9/8
Mercury Topaz '91	$400 (C) or Plan 4 and 5% of list price (D)	9/23
Mercury Topaz '92	$500 (C) or Plan 4	9/23
Mitsubishi Galant '91/'92	$0–$1,200 (D)	9/30
Mitsubishi '91/'92 (pickup)	$0–$1,200 (D)	9/30
Nissan Stanza '92 (except w/F09 package)	$1,500–$2,000 (D) based on sales targets set for individual dealer	9/2
Nissan Stanza '92 (w/F09 package)	$1,500–$3,431 (D) based on sales targets set for individual dealer (varies by region)	9/2
Oldsmobile Achieva '92	$750 (C) or Plan 3	9/23
Peugeot 405 '91	$5,000 (D)	not set
Plymouth Acclaim '91/'92	$1,000 (C) or Plan 2	8/31
Plymouth Sundance '91/'92	$700 (C) or Plan 2	8/31
Pontiac Grand Am '92	$500 (C) or Plan 1	9/23
Pontiac LeMans '92	$1,000 (D)	9/23
Pontiac Sunbird '92	$0 (C) or ($500 [C] or Plan 1) (varies by region)	9/23
Saab 900 '92	Plan 7 (C)	8/30
Subaru Legacy '92 (L+AWD invoiced after 2/3)	$1,500 (D)	11/3
		(continued)

Model	Cash to Customer (C) or Dealer (D) and/or Finance Plan (plans below)	End
COMPACT CARS (cont.)		
Subaru Legacy '92 (L+AWD invoiced before 2/4)	$1,000 (D)	11/3
Subaru Legacy '92 (L+FWD invoiced after 2/3)	$1,000 (D)	11/3
Subaru Legacy '92 (L+FWD invoiced before 2/4)	$500 (D)	11/3
Subaru Legacy '92 (LS AWD invoiced after 2/3)	$2,700 (D)	11/3
Subaru Legacy '92 (LS AWD invoiced before 2/4)	$2,200 (D)	11/3
Subaru Legacy '92 (LS FWD invoiced after 2/3)	$2,500 (D)	11/3
Subaru Legacy '92 (LS FWD invoiced before 2/4)	$2,000 (D)	11/3
Subaru Legacy '92 (L invoiced after 2/3)	$1,000 (D)	11/3
Subaru Legacy '92 (L invoiced before 2/4)	$500 (D)	11/3
Volkswagen Cabriolet '92	$1,500 (D)	9/30
Volkswagen Corrado '92	$1,500 (D)	9/30
Volkswagen Jetta '92 (except GLI, diesel), Golf (except diesel), and Fox	$500 (D)	9/30
Volkswagen Passat '92	$750 (D)	9/30
MIDSIZE CARS		
Buick Century '92	$250–$1,000 (C) or Plan 3 ($250 w/package SA or SB; $500 w/package SC; $750 w/package SD or SM; $1,000 w/package SE or SF)	9/23
Buick Regal '92	$500–$1,250 (C) or Plan 3 ($750 w/package SA or SB; $1,000 w/package SC; $1,250 w/package SD or SM; $1,500 w/package SE or SF)	9/23
Buick Riviera '92	$2,000 (C) or Plan 3	9/23
Chevrolet Caprice '92	$500 (C) or Plan 5	9/23
Chevrolet Lumina '92 (coupe and sedan)	$1,500 (C) or Plan 5	9/23
Chrysler Imperial '91/'92	$1,500 (C) or Plan 2; and $1,000–$2,000 (D) based on sales targets set for individual dealer	8/31
Chrysler Imperial '93	$1,250 (C) or Plan 2	8/31
Chrysler New Yorker Fifth Avenue '91/'92	$1,500 (C) or Plan 2; and $1,000–$2,000 (D) based on sales targets set for individual dealer	8/31
Chrysler New Yorker Fifth Avenue '93	$1,250 (C) or Plan 2	8/31
Chrysler New Yorker Salon '91/'92	$1,000 (C) or Plan 2; and $1,000–$2,000 (D) based on sales targets set for individual dealer	8/31

(continued)

Model	Cash to Customer (C) or Dealer (D) and/or Finance Plan (plans below)	End
MIDSIZE CARS (cont.)		
Chrysler New Yorker Salon '93	$750 (C) or Plan 2	8/31
Dodge Dynasty '91/'92	$1,000 (C) or Plan 2	8/31
Dodge Dynasty '93	$750 (C) or Plan 2	8/31
Eagle Premier '91/'92	$1,500 (C) or Plan 2	8/31
Ford Taurus '91 (except SHO)	$400–$1,000 (C) (varies by region) or Plan 4 and 5% of list price (D)	9/23
Ford Taurus '91 SHO	$600 (C) or Plan 4 and 5% of list price (D) (plus $1,000–$3,000 [D] for "demo" models)	9/23
Ford Taurus '92 (except SHO)	$750–$1,000 (C) or Plan 4 plus $0–$180 (D)** based on sales targets set for individual dealer (varies by region)	9/23
Ford Taurus '92 SHO	$1,000 (C) or Plan 4 (plus $1,000–$2,000 [D] for "demo" models)	9/23
Ford Thunderbird '91	$750 (C) or Plan 4 and 5% of list price (D)	9/23
Ford Thunderbird '92	$0–$1,500 (C) or Plan 4 (varies by state)	9/23
Hyundai Sonata '91	$2,000 (C)	10/2
Hyundai Sonata '92 (with V6 engine)	$2,000 (C)	10/2
Hyundai Sonata '92 (without V6 engine)	$1,500 (C)	10/2
Jaguar XJ-S, XJ6, Sovereign, and Vanden Plas '91	$3,000–$8,000 (D)	8/15
Lincoln Continental '92	$2,000 (C)	9/23
Lincoln Mark VII '92	$3,000 (C)	9/23
Mercedes-Benz '91 SE, 300SEL, 350SD, and 350SDL	$3,000 (D)	not set
Mercury Cougar '91	$750 (C) or Plan 4 and 5% of list price (D)	9/23
Mercury Cougar '92	$0–$1,500 (C) or Plan 4 (varies by state)	9/23
Mercury Sable '91	$400 (C) or Plan 4 and 5% of list price (D)	9/23
Mercury Sable '92	$750–$1,000 (C) or Plan 4 (varies by state)	9/23
Nissan Maxima '92 (GXE)	$1,000–$1,500 (D) based on sales targets set for individual dealer	9/2
Nissan Maxima '92 (SE)	$500–$1,000 (D) based on sales targets set for individual dealer	9/2
Oldsmobile Cutlass Ciera '92	$1,000 (C) or Plan 3	9/23
Oldsmobile Cutlass Supreme '92	$500–$1,250 (C) (varies by region) or Plan 3	9/23
Oldsmobile Toronado '92	$500–$2,500 (C) (varies by region) or Plan 3	9/23
Peugeot 505 '91	$6,000 (D)	not set
Pontiac Grand Prix '92	$500–$750 (C) (varies by region) or Plan 1	9/23
Saab 9000 '92	Plan 7 (C)	8/30
LARGE CARS		
Buick LeSabre '92	$250–$1,000 (C) or Plan 3 ($250 w/package SA or SB; $500 w/package SC; $750 w/package SD or SM; $1,000 w/package SE or SF)	9/23
Buick Park Avenue '92 (incl. Ultra)	$1,000 (C) or Plan 3	9/23

(continued)

Model	Cash to Customer (C) or Dealer (D) and/or Finance Plan (plans below)	End
LARGE CARS (cont.)		
Buick Roadmaster '92	$1,000 (C) or Plan 3	9/23
Cadillac Brougham '92	$1,500 (C)	9/23
Cadillac De Ville '92	$1,500 (C)	9/23
Cadillac Fleetwood '92	$1,500 (C)	9/23
Ford Crown Victoria '91	$1,000 (D) plus 5% of list price (D)	9/23
Ford Crown Victoria '92	$500 (C) or Plan 4	9/23
Lincoln Town Car '92	$2,000 (C)	9/23
Mercedes-Benz '91 420SEL and 560SEL	$5,000 (D)	not set
Mercury Grand Marquis '92	$500 (C) or Plan 4	9/23
Oldsmobile Custom Cruiser '92	$500–$2,000 or Plan 3 (varies by region)	9/23
Oldsmobile Eighty-Eight '92	$500–$1,000 (C) (varies by region) or Plan 3	9/23
Oldsmobile Ninety-Eight '92	$1,500 (C) or Plan 3; and $1,500 (D) (Washington, DC zone)	9/23
Pontiac Bonneville '92	$750 (C) or Plan 1	9/23
SMALL VANS		
Chevrolet Astro '92	$500 (C) or Plan 5	9/23
Chevrolet G-Van '92 (non-32 models with Y57 package)	$1,300 (C) or Plan 5	9/23
Chevrolet G-Van '92 (non-32 models without Y57 package)	$500 (C) or Plan 5	9/23
Chevrolet Lumina '92 APV	$750 (C) or Plan 5	9/23
Chrysler Town and Country '91/'92 (long wheel-base)	$500 (C) or Plan 2 (residents CA, HI only)	8/31
Chrysler Town and Country '91/'92 (short wheel-base)	$500 (C) or Plan 2; plus special equipment discounts (except residents CA, HI)	8/31
Dodge Caravan '91/'92 (long wheel-base)	$0–$500 (C) (varies by state) or Plan 2; plus special equipment discounts	8/31
Dodge Caravan '91/'92 (short wheel-base)	$500 (C) or Plan 2; plus special equipment discounts	8/31
Dodge Ram '91/'92/'93 (wagon, van, conversion)	$1,000 (C) or Plan 2	8/31
Ford Aerostar '91	$400–$1,000 (C) or Plan 4 (varies by region) and 5% of list price (D)	9/23
Ford Aerostar '92	$500–$1,000 (C) or Plan 4 (varies by region)	9/23
Ford Econoline '91 (with E-150 RV package)	$1,000 (C) or Plan 4 and 5% of list price (D)	9/23
Ford Econoline '91 (without E-150 RV package)	$400 (C) or Plan 4 and 5% of list price (D)	9/23
Ford Econoline '92 (with RV package)	$1,000 (C) or Plan 4	9/23
GMC G-Van '92 (non-32 models with Y57 package)	$1,300 (C) or Plan 1	9/23
GMC G-Van '92 (non-32 models without Y57 package)	$500 (C) or Plan 1	9/23

(continued)

Model	Cash to Customer (C) or Dealer (D) and/or Finance Plan (plans below)	End
SMALL VANS (cont.)		
GMC Safari '92	$500 (C) or Plan 1	9/23
Mazda MPV '92	$1,000 (C)	9/8
Oldsmobile Silhouette '92	$500–$1,000 (C) or Plan 3 (varies by region)	9/23
Plymouth Voyager '91/'92 (long wheel-base)	$500 (C) or Plan 2 (residents CA, HI only)	8/31
Plymouth Voyager '91/'92 (short wheel-base)	$500 (C) or Plan 2; plus special equipment discounts (except residents, CA, HI)	8/31
Pontiac Trans Sport '92	$750 (C) or Plan 1	9/23
PICKUPS		
Chevrolet S-10 '92 pickup	$750 (C) or Plan 5	9/23
Dodge Dakota '91/'92	$500 (C) or Plan 2	8/31
Dodge Ram 50 '91/'92	$500 (C) or Plan 2	8/31
Dodge Ram '91/'92/'93 pickup (gas)	$1,500 (C) or Plan 2	8/31
Ford F-Series '91 pickup	$400 (C) or Plan 4 plus 5% of list price (D)	9/23
Ford F-Series '92 pickup	$300 (C) or Plan 4 plus $0–$180 (D)** based on sales targets set for individual dealer	9/23
Ford Ranger '91	$400 (C) or Plan 4 and 5% of list price (D)	9/23
Ford Ranger '92 (except Flareside)	$750–$1,000 (C) or Plan 4 (varies by state)	9/23
GMC Sierra '92 (except Crew Cab and Extended Cab)	$400 (C) or Plan 1	9/23
GMC Sonoma '92	$750 (C) or Plan 1	9/23
Isuzu pickup Q16 '91/'92	$800–$1,600 (D)	9/30
Mazda pickup '92	$0–$1,400 (C) (varies by region)	9/8
Nissan '92 pickup (except base)	$1,300 (D) based on sales targets set for individual dealer	9/2
Nissan '92/'93 pickup (base models)	$1,000 (D) based on sales targets set for individual dealer	9/2
Nissan '93 pickup (except base)	$750 (D) based on sales targets set for individual dealer	9/2
Toyota pickup '91/'92 (base models)	$800–$1,200 (D) based on sales targets set for individual dealer	9/2
Toyota pickup '91/'92 (non-base models)	$300–$500 (D) based on sales targets set for individual dealer	9/2
SPORT/UTILITY VEHICLES		
Chevrolet S-10 '92 Blazer	$2,000 (C) or Plan 5	9/23
Dodge Ramcharger '91/'92	$2,000 (C) or Plan 2	8/31
Ford Bronco '91	$1,000 (C) or Plan 4 and 5% of list price (D)	9/23
Ford Bronco '92	$1,000 (C) or Plan 4	9/23
GMC Jimmy '92 (except Typhoon)	$2,000 (C) or Plan 1	9/23
Geo Tracker '92 (2WD models)	$750 (C) or Plan 5	9/23
Geo Tracker '92 (4WD models)	$1,000 (C) or Plan 5	9/23

(continued)

Model	Cash to Customer (C) or Dealer (D) and/or Finance Plan (plans below)	End
SPORT/UTILITY VEHICLES (cont.)		
Isuzu Rodeo '91/'92 (2WD)	$400 (D)	9/30
Isuzu Rodeo '91/'92 (4WD)	$950 (D) or $800–$1,400 (D) (dealer chooses)	9/30
Jeep Cherokee '91/'92	$1,500 (C) or Plan 2 and $750 (D)	8/31
Jeep Cherokee '93	$500 (C) or Plan 2	8/31
Jeep Comanche '91/'92	$500 (C) or Plan 2	8/31
Jeep Wrangler '91/'92	$500 (C) or Plan 2	8/31
Mazda Navajo '92	$0–$1,500 (C) (varies by region)	9/8
Nissan Pathfinder '92	$1,000 (D)	9/2
Oldsmobile Bravada '92	$500–$2,000 (C) (varies by region) or Plan 3	9/23
Plymouth Vista '91/'92	$500 (C) or Plan 2	8/31
Suzuki Sidekick '92 (2-dr JS, JX, LE)	$1,000 (D) or (C)	10/2
Suzuki Sidekick '92 (4-dr JS, JX, JLX)	$700 (D) or (C)	10/2
Suzuki Sidekick '92 (4-dr LTD)	$1,000 (D) or (C)	10/2
Suzuki Sidekick '93 (2-dr)	$600 (D) or (C)	10/2
Suzuki Sidekick '93 (4-dr)	$300 (D) or (C)	10/2
SPORTY CARS		
Cadillac Allante '91	$7,500–$8,500 (D)	9/23
Chevrolet Beretta '92	$500 (C) or Plan 5	9/23
Chevrolet Camaro '92	$500 (C) or Plan 5	9/23
Chevrolet Corvette '92 (except ZR-1)	$1,000 (D)	9/23
Chevrolet Corvette '92 ZR-1	$2,000 (D)	9/23
Dodge Daytona '91	$1,500 (C) or Plan 2	8/31
Dodge Daytona '92/'93	$1,000 (C) or Plan 2	8/31
Eagle Talon '91/'92 (all-wheel drive models)	$1,500 (C) or Plan 2	8/31
Eagle Talon '91/'92 (except all-wheel drive models)	$1,000 (C) or Plan 2	8/31
Ford Mustang '91	$750 (C) or Plan 4 and 5% of list price (D)	9/23
Ford Mustang '92	$500–$1,000 (C) or Plan 4 (varies by state)	9/23
Ford Probe '91	$1,000 (C) or Plan 4 and 5% of list price (D)	9/23
Ford Probe '92	$1,500 (C) or Plan 4 and 5% of list price (D)	9/23
Geo Storm '91/'92	$1,500 (C) or Plan 5	9/23
Hyundai Scoupe '91 (non-SE models)	$1,500 (C)	10/2
Hyundai Scoupe '91 (SE models)	$1,000 (C)	10/2
Hyundai Scoupe '92 (LS)	$750 (C)	10/2
Hyundai Scoupe '92 (L)	$500 (C)	10/2
Isuzu Impulse '91	$2,500 (D)	9/30
Isuzu Impulse '92	$1,500 (D)	9/30
Isuzu Stylus '91 S	$800 (D)	9/30
Isuzu Stylus '91 XS	$1,100 (D)	9/30
Isuzu Stylus '92 S and RS	$500 (D)	9/30
Mazda MX-6 '92	$1,400 (C)	9/8
Mazda RX-7 '91	$2,000 (D)	9/8

(continued)

Model	Cash to Customer (C) or Dealer (D) and/or Finance Plan (plans below)	End
SPORTY CARS (cont.)		
Mercury Capri '91	$2,000 (C) or Plan 4 and 5% of list price (D)	9/23
Mercury Capri '92 (except XR-2)	$1,000 (C) or Plan 4	9/23
Mercury Capri '92 (XR-2)	$1,500 (C) or Plan 4	9/23
Mercury Capri '93	$500 (C) or Plan 4	9/23
Mitsubishi Eclipse '91/'92	$0–$1,200 (D)	9/30
Nissan 240SX '92 (except convertible)	$1,200–$1,700 (D) based on sales targets set for individual dealer	9/2
Nissan 300ZX '92 (except convertible)	$1,000–$2,000 (D) based on sales targets set for individual dealer	9/2
Plymouth Laser '91/'92 (all-wheel drive models)	$1,500 (C) or Plan 2	8/31
Plymouth Laser '91/'92 (except all-wheel drive models)	$1,000 (C) or Plan 2	8/31
Pontiac Firebird '92	$750–$1,000 (C) (varies by region) or Plan 1	9/23
Subaru SVX '92	$2,000 (D)	11/3
Toyota Celica '92	$600–$800 (D) based on sales targets set for individual dealer	9/2

**If dealer meets targets by end of period, gets cash for all cars sold in period.

Finance Plans:
Plan 1 = 6.9% APR up to 48 mos. (3.9% APR up to 48 mos. available on Grand Am and Bonneville—also Sunbird in some states.)
Plan 2 = 4.9% APR up to 24 mos., 6.9% up to 36 mos., 7.9% up to 48 mos., 9.9% up to 60 mos. (Minivans: 6.9% APR up to 24 mos., 7.9% APR up to 36 mos., 8.9% APR up to 48 mos., 9.9% APR up to 60 mos. Lower rates may be available on some models which vary by region.)
Plan 3 = 2.9% APR up to 24 mos., 4.9% APR up to 36 mos., 6.9% APR up to 48 mos. (2.9% APR up to 24 mos., 3.9% up to 48 mos. available on Achieva, Cutlass Supreme, Regal, Skylark.)
Plan 4 = 7.9% APR up to 48 mos. (Lower rates may be available on some models which vary by region.)
Plan 5 = 6.9% APR up to 48 mos. (2.9% APR up to 48 mos. available on GEO.)
Plan 6 = 0.0% APR up to 48 mos. with 40% down payment
Plan 7 = 3.9% APR up to 48 mos. with 25% down payment
Plan 8 = 5.9% APR up to 60 mos. (Lower rates may be available on some models which vary by region.)

DOLLAR SAVINGS PER $1,000 of LOAN AMOUNT

Prevailing Market Rate (APR)	Dealer's Factory-Subsidized Interest Rate						
	3%	4%	5%	6%	7%	8%	9%
2-Year Loan							
7%	40.01	30.10	20.13	10.09	—	—	—
8%	49.66	39.85	29.98	20.05	10.05	—	—
9%	59.18	49.47	39.69	29.86	19.97	10.01	—
10%	68.56	58.94	49.27	39.53	29.74	19.89	9.97
11%	77.81	68.29	58.71	49.07	39.38	29.62	19.81
12%	86.93	77.51	68.02	58.48	48.88	39.22	29.50
13%	95.93	86.60	77.20	67.76	58.25	46.68	39.06
14%	104.80	95.56	86.26	76.90	67.49	58.02	48.49
15%	113.55	104.39	95.19	85.92	76.60	67.22	57.79
3-Year Loan	3%	4%	5%	6%	7%	8%	9%
7%	58.16	43.82	29.35	14.74	—	—	—
8%	71.97	57.84	43.57	29.18	14.66	—	—
9%	85.49	71.56	57.51	48.33	29.01	14.57	—
10%	98.74	85.01	71.16	57.19	43.08	28.85	14.49
11%	111.72	98.19	84.54	70.77	56.86	42.83	28.68
12%	124.44	111.11	97.65	84.07	70.37	56.54	42.59
13%	136.90	123.76	110.50	97.11	83.60	69.97	56.22
14%	149.11	136.16	123.08	109.89	96.57	83.13	69.57
15%	161.09	148.31	135.42	122.41	109.28	96.03	82.66
4-Year Loan	3%	4%	5%	6%	7%	8%	9%
7%	75.67	57.09	38.29	19.26	—	—	—
8%	93.34	75.12	56.68	38.01	19.12	—	—
9%	110.54	92.67	74.57	56.26	37.73	18.97	—
10%	127.28	109.75	92.00	74.03	55.84	37.44	18.83
11%	143.59	126.38	108.96	91.33	73.49	55.43	37.16
12%	159.47	142.58	125.49	108.18	90.67	72.94	55.02
13%	174.94	158.36	141.58	124.59	107.40	90.00	72.41
14%	190.00	173.73	157.25	140.57	123.70	106.62	89.34
15%	204.68	188.70	172.52	156.15	139.58	122.81	105.84

(continued)

Prevailing Market Rate (APR)	Dealer's Factory-Subsidized Interest Rate						
	3%	4%	5%	6%	7%	8%	9%
5-Year Loan							
7%	92.55	69.93	46.97	23.65	—	—	—
8%	113.81	91.73	69.30	46.54	23.44	—	—
9%	134.39	112.81	90.91	68.67	46.11	23.22	—
10%	154.30	133.22	111.82	90.09	68.05	45.68	23.00
11%	173.57	152.97	132.05	110.83	89.28	67.43	45.26
12%	192.22	172.08	151.64	130.89	109.84	88.47	66.81
13%	210.27	190.59	170.61	150.32	129.74	108.85	87.67
14%	227.76	208.51	188.97	169.13	149.00	128.58	107.87
15%	244.69	225.87	206.76	187.35	167.66	147.69	127.43

Index

customer satisfaction index (CSI), 112–13
disappearing, 56–59
F&I managers, 38, 101–2
financing through, 38–39
house sales, 147–50
impact of losing, 57
inventories of, 99–100
license plate frames, 98, 111
location of, 107
logos on cars, 98
mega-, 112
negotiating with, 120–27
"no dicker," 64–68
numbers of cars sold, 2
picking finalists, 106–15
price discrimination by, 6, 7–9
price vs. service, 106–7
profit motive, 2–3
and regular customers, 110–11
service departments, 107–11
shopping your used car at, 27–28
special orders, 98–100
trade-ins, 24–25
used-car departments, 27–30
and warranty repairs, 107, 108–11
window stickers, 48, 96
see also factory-to-dealer incentives
demand vs. supply, 10–11, 119
deposit checks, 93–94
depreciation
defined, 133–34
and leasing, 136, 137–38, 139, 142
destination charge, 72
disappearing car companies, 53–56
disappearing dealers, 56–59
discrimination, *see* price discrimination
Dodge
family relations, 50
Viper, 10, 112
down payment
deciding on, 39, 41
in leasing, 134–35

Eagle, 50, 54
80/20 rule, 19–20
emotional detachment, 15

end-of-year leftovers, 84–86, 119
equity borrowing, 43
extended warranties
as back-end profit items, 101–2
negotiating price, 104–5, 128
tips on, 104–5
when to purchase, 104, 128
whether to purchase, 104

fabric protection, 97
factory orders, 98–100
factory-to-customer incentives, 75, 77–79
listed in *CarDeals*, 77, 176–82
rebates vs. financing, 78, 183–84
factory-to-dealer incentives, 76–77, 79–80
defined, 70
listed in *CarDeals*, 77, 175–82
using in negotiation, 119, 125
family relations, 49–50
Fighting Chance package
Big Picture, 158
CarDeals issue, 158–59
dealer invoice price data, 159
elements of, 157–58
how to order, 161–62
sample information, 169–82
F&I managers
and extended warranties, 101–2
and financing, 38
financing
average new car loan, 42
avoiding "upside down," 40
calculations, 41
comparison shopping for, 40–43
deciding on down payment, 39, 41
determining monthly payment, 39, 41
as factory-to-customer incentive, 78
vs. leasing, 137–39
market APRs vs. dealer-subsidized, 78, 183–84
shopping for, 39
telephone research, 40–41
through dealer, 38–39
20 percent down/four-year rule, 40, 41
using home equity loan, 43
when to bring up, 117, 128

About the Author

W. James Bragg could name every car on the road when he was three years old, long before he could read. As a teenager his car fancy was fueled by a fire-engine red 1962 Ford convertible, and he's been an avid student of the automotive world ever since.

In the 1970s he was marketing vp of an automotive company that sold accessories nobody needed, but everybody wanted—items like chrome-plated air cleaners and the "surfer" foot pedal, a barefoot-shaped pad that attached to the accelerator and made every kid feel like one of the Beach Boys.

Today he's down to two passions. Fortunately, one of them is analyzing what's happening in the automotive market and determining what it means for new car and truck shoppers. That's what *In the Driver's Seat* is all about.